walkers, bums; and

...MPSEY
...HE MAN HIMSELF

As Told to

BOB CONSIDINE and BILL SLOCUM

H 8321

SIMON AND SCHUSTER • NEW YORK • 1960

LIBRARY OF CONGRESS CATALOG CARD NUMBER: 60-6719
MANUFACTURED IN THE UNITED STATES OF AMERICA
BY H. WOLFF, NEW YORK.

FROM **DEMPSEY**

Saloon fighting at 16: When things were real tough I'd walk into a strange saloon and say, like a skinny John L. Sullivan, "I can lick any man in the house." Unlike John L., who had a lot of class, I guess, I'd add, "For a buck." I weighed 130. It got me a lot of fights.

❋

Firpo: I have no memory to this day of the most spectacular thing that ever happened to me in my fighting life—being knocked out of the ring by Firpo. I backed up as he came on, trading punches. I was instinctively waiting for my back to touch the ropes, I guess. But just before I could touch, and with about ten seconds left of the first round, he half hit and half shoved me with a right to the face.

I went out of the ring backward, between the top and middle ropes, and landed on my neck on Jack Lawrence's typewriter in the first row of the press section. I don't remember getting back into the ring. In the second I went after him again. I stuck a right under his left hand and finally crossed him on the chin. He was swaying like a ship at sea. Two good lefts to the jaw, and that was all there was to it.

❋

The one man Dempsey feared: Many have written of my "killer instinct," my "fighting heart." I was small as heavyweights go and usually fought giants, so they called me "Jack the Giant Killer." They said I feared no man. The hell I feared no man! There was one man—he was even smaller than I—I wouldn't fight because I knew he would flatten me. I was afraid of Sam Langford.

❋

1922: That year was for laughs. In the spring a bunch of us went to Europe. The only time I came close to a ring was one night I refereed a fight in Paris. There wasn't much doubt in my mind who the winner would be. I climbed into the ring, held up the hand of a guy named Billy Balzac and yelled "Le victor, Monsewer Billy Balzac." I wasn't sure whether he won or not. But the other guy's name was Maurice Proxineaux or something like that. How the hell could I have given it to him? Georges Carpentier joined me in the ring and put his arm around my shoulders. "Jack," he said, "if you had a right hand like your French accent I'd be heavyweight champion of the world."

THIS BOOK *is dedicated to my daughters
... and their daughters.
God love them. He sure did me.*

*A section of photographs will be found
following page 122.*

I AM WILLIAM HARRISON DEMPSEY, A Jack Mormon, ex-heavyweight-champion of the world, rich in friends, richer in loved ones, comfortable in the world's goods.

I am sixty-four. I haven't been champion for a third of a century, yet I'm recognized wherever I go. Kids and grownups greet me with affection anywhere in the land.

This book should tell why I'm so grateful for that affection. I didn't have it when I was champion of the world. And I wanted it so very much.

This is my book. It's the record I leave for my daughters, Joan and Barbara, and for my grandchildren. So, as I know the truth, this will be a true book.

I'm told that eight books have been written about me. One of them I never finished reading, five or six I never even attempted to start. But I've read and reread every word that follows. I didn't enjoy reading some of them. But they give the honest answers to the questions I was asked.

They tell me this is Horatio Alger stuff. (I never read Horatio Alger.) Rags to riches, ruthless villains, all the tears any man needs, misunderstanding, disgrace, triumph.

Plus a few things Mr. Alger didn't go in for: beautiful movie and stage stars, a lot of laughs, pressure groups, knocking good guys senseless as a way of life, war, suicide, divorce.

This is work. I worked harder to produce it than anybody else connected with it.

Why didn't I turn over the record books and the scrapbooks to a competent man and just sit back? Here are some reasons why:

Others have written of my "killer instinct," my "fighting heart"; some even say I was the greatest fighter of my century. They were impressed by my courage in the ring. I was small as heavyweights go and usually fought giants, so they called me "Jack the Giant Killer." They said I feared no man.

The hell I feared no man! There was one man— he was even smaller than I— I wouldn't fight because I knew he would flatten me. I was afraid of Sam Langford.

They said I was a bum. A wild, untamed kid who came swinging out of the Wild West to fight in saloons, ride the rods, make a buck any way I could.

What is a bum? If being badly educated, owning one ragged shirt and a pair of patched pants and having holes in my shoes makes a man a bum, I was a bum.

But I went hungry for days rather than steal. I begged, humbly, for any kind of job to earn a flop and a meal.

I never was a bum bum.

I was a starving kid, wandering in search of food, sometimes almost like an animal, living as best I could and with the weapons of survival God gave me. My fists. And I guess my chin.

Ever hustle a sucker?

I sure did.

Been hustled pretty good, too. I'm possibly the leading sucker of my time.

I've read serious studies on what made me the great fighter they say I was. All agreed it was the natural result of poverty, the rough life on the last American frontier, and the fact that I had to fight to survive and thereby accidentally learned that I could fight better than I could do anything else.

Bunk.

There was no future in a hundred of the itinerant-workers' jobs I had. But I could have made a life's work out of two of these jobs— as a cowboy or as a miner. I was pretty good at both. I enjoyed mining, believe it or not, and I dug for everything you can dig for in these United States, from coal to gold— and even uranium before it was used for what it's used today.

Who is to say I wouldn't have been happier had I been a rancher or a mine operator?

But I was never anything, really, except a fighter. That's all I ever wanted to be. When I was eleven I was in serious training to win the heavyweight championship of the world. I wasn't surprised when I became champion thirteen brutal years later.

But, in those thirteen years, there were many moments and many months when I wondered. . . .

A natural-born killer, they said.

But of all the men I have beaten or who have beaten me I disliked Carl Morris.

Jack Kearns?

I have no love for Jack Kearns.

Jack Kearns was a brilliant manager, the best I ever had— maybe the best any fighter ever had. I freely confess a great debt to him. But insist that he more than saw to it that said debt was paid.

Many said I was ruthless in the ring. How I'd stand over a fellow who was down and clout him again as he tried to rise. How I would get behind an opponent staggering back to his feet and flatten him with a sucker punch as he turned to face me.

Guilty!

I did those things and more. And did them well. Why shouldn't I have been adept at such tactics? I had learned all those tricks from men who flattened me again as I struggled for footing. Or threw brain-shaking sucker rights as I turned groggily to face them. It was part of the rules— or lack of rules— through many of my ring years.

I've been beaten into a coma in rings. I've been knocked down too often to remember. I've been knocked out. That happens to everybody if he lives in a jungle long enough. But I never lost a fight on a foul. Nor was I ever thrown out of a ring for not trying.

Women. I love women. An awful lot of women have been kind and generous, and magnificent company.

I married three times. But each was a disaster.

Old friends of the carefree twenties, some of them sports columnists, get weepy or surprised because I call my daughters almost every day, no matter where I am in the world. And because I fly thousands of miles for no other reason than to play with my granddaughters. (Five, as we go to press.)

These old pals are astonished at the picture of "the

Manassa Mauler," "Jack the Giant Killer," the man with the famed "killer instinct" in the role of a doting family man.

I traveled thousands of miles— on the rods— to say hello to my mother, a strong, closemouthed but witty woman I adored. I rode the rods to bury a kid brother stabbed in the streets of Salt Lake City.

I was fond of my father, and that could be difficult.

I loved and still love family life and the happiness and sorrow that are always part of it. I just never happened to have much of it. Believe me, I tried. I tried so hard.

I graduated from the eighth grade of the Lakeview School in Utah, largely for the convenience of the teacher. I must have driven him daffy.

For many years now the American people have shown they like me. Shown it in a thousand and more ways. Flattering ways. And ways, frankly, that have been personally most lucrative.

But once these same American people hated me as damn few Americans have ever been hated by their own countrymen.

The United States Government has said, officially, that I was a slacker. It has also said, officially, that I was worthy of the Legion of Merit.

The United States Government was wrong both times.

Being heavyweight champion of the world is a wonderful experience for any man. I got more out of it than any man before or after me. I was lucky— the right guy at the right time.

I knew some of the Presidents and met some of the kings in the last forty years. Also a lot of the most beautiful women, the renowned hoodlums, and bank presidents who would have rung the burglar alarm if I had walked in on them once upon a time.

I'm sure I'm glad I won that championship.

But would my beloved brother Johnny, the favorite of all who met him, have taken to dope and killed his wonderful wife and himself if he hadn't been "the champ's brother" in the days when Hollywood was at its wildest and Wally Reid, the star who died of narcotics, was proud to shake Johnny's hand?

Would an editor I had refused a favor gain his revenge by smearing me with the word "slacker" had I been anybody but the heavyweight champion of the world?

Would two of the women I loved have married me if I had been less than heavyweight champion of the world or an honored ex-champion? And could I have been able to make them happy if I were capable of spending more time with them? There was so much money to be made. But always away from home. And I must always roam, I have to.

Would I have been in so many law courts? If I had entered some milder business than boxing would I have been so thoroughly fleeced? Would I have known the sick feeling of being all washed up in my chosen profession and finding I was broke after making millions?

And the broken ribs . . . the ear hanging by a shred . .

the fighter pal who was dying and had to be flattened for his own good . . . the spine injury that never healed, often hurt . . . the managers?

I guess the rewards were greater than the penalties and the pain.

I'm almost sure they were.

Let's see, then, what really happened— and I never did learn how to pull a punch.

CHAPTER **2**

IN 1915, WHEN I WAS NINETEEN, I fought Johnny Sudenberg ten rounds in the wild mining town of Goldfield, Nevada. I was in there with a good fighter, one much better than I was, but I took the fight because I was dead broke and my manager of the moment, Jack Gilfeather, had been able to jimmy a $100 guarantee out of a promoter named Jake Goodfriend. Jake promised all that money because Sudenberg's scheduled opponent had taken a runout.

Sudenberg almost killed me. For two rounds it was a fight. For the next eight I was a helpless, blood-soaked punching bag. It was the worst beating of my life. I don't remember going down once, because I still don't remember the last three or four rounds.

Goldfield was a tough town. A stranger who got his brains knocked out in Goldfield was no rarity. Hardly worth bothering a doctor about. So they dumped me, unconscious, into a wheelbarrow and some Samaritan pushed me through the hilly streets. He threw me on the bunk in my "home." I slept.

My "home" was a cave in the side of a hill. Goldfield had been a boom mining town and a room cost five dollars a week. In advance, for a skinny young hobo with holes in his shoes and a newspaper for a suitcase.

There must have been much unconsciousness mixed with that sleep, because I remember nothing until I woke up at three o'clock the next afternoon — nearly twenty hours after I'd been wheelbarrowed "home." Everything hurt, of course. But I was young, and I was hungry. I stumbled over to the saloon where Gilfeather hung out, to collect my share of the purse.

In the saloon a few heroes laughed at my battered face. A few made jokes about how funny I looked being trundled through the streets in a wheelbarrow (which is the way I found out about that journey).

I asked where I could find Gilfeather.

A bartender said, "He left town last night, kid. He got drunk and blew his wad shooting craps."

I had been damn near killed for nothing. I was broke and starving. It was the lowest point of my entire life. And, for the first time in my life, I longed for my childhood, tough as it was.

It had been a rugged childhood. An old story, perhaps, but a painful one: too many mouths to feed, a father with the wanderlust and almost no ability to make a decent living, a mother who performed all a wife's chores and saw to all a husband's responsibilities. It was the kind of life that had sent me on the road as soon as I could get away. As it had sent my older brothers and sisters.

I was born June 24, 1895, in Manassa, Colorado, the ninth child and the fifth son of Hyrum and Cecilia Smoot Dempsey. I am basically Irish, with Cherokee blood from both parents, plus a Jewish strain from my father's great-grandmother, Rachel Solomon.

A lot of people have said the Indian showed more in me than it did in my eight older brothers and sisters or in the boy and girl who were born after me. I have the high cheekbones, the jet-black hair of an Indian. There's some gray in the hair today and some fat around the cheekbones, but I still walk with the Indian's pigeon-toed glide.

Oddly, my always hard-up parents had come from well-to-do families. Cecilia Smoot's father had owned a prosperous grocery store in Tazewell, Virginia. Hyrum Dempsey's father was a big landowner and a major politician in Logan County, West Virginia. He was sheriff and county surveyor of Logan for years.

My mother was born around 1856, my father a little sooner. I remember him telling of hiding in the woods during the Civil War. I don't know when or where my parents met— they weren't the kind to go in for romantic reminiscences. But when my oldest brother, Bernie, was born they were living in Logan County. Bernie was born twenty years before I was, or in 1875, so my mother may have been seventeen or eighteen when she married.

She was a small woman— never weighed more than 110. Her light-blue eyes sparkled in a pale face below jet-black hair. My old man towered over her. He was a wiry six feet one inch. Weighed maybe 150 pounds. No more. And there was no doubt in the world where I got my high, almost girlish, voice. Right from him.

My mother was the most magnificent human being I ever met. I knew that before I was ten. I was a mamma's boy when I was a kid. I enjoyed helping her with the washing and the cooking. I knew from the time I could walk that she deserved a better break. And I swore or vowed or prayed or whatever it is a kid does that I would someday make it up to her.

I think I understand my father better now than I did in Colorado, Utah, West Virginia and points in between. He was a confused man. He actually had a full year of college. He wouldn't talk much about it but I think it was in Cincinnati. He was, by trade, a schoolteacher. But he hated teachers and he despised his job at Mud Fork, West Virginia. He quit teaching, and no matter how bad our luck was after that he wouldn't enter another schoolhouse.

There couldn't be much happiness for an educated man in Logan County, then one of the roughest, toughest areas in our land. It was coal country, and a man who didn't dig or plant but taught was doing woman's work. A reader was a fool and a dreamer. Besides, there was nothing to read in Logan.

My father got religion in Logan. Got it after he had sired a son and a daughter. A Mormon missionary told him of his faith. I'm sure the intelligence and humanity of the Mormon beliefs appealed to him. Getting out of Logan appealed, also.

My mother and father became Mormons. But he was a Jack Mormon almost immediately, one who doesn't live by the book. He drank, smoked, took coffee, and violated 'most all the laws of a faith he believed in fundamentally. Pop could explain this contradiction. He'd grin and say, "I know the church is right. I'm just too weak to live up to those rules."

My mother was a real Mormon, from the day she embraced the faith until the day she died in 1943.

Her death tells a lot about her life. She was attended in her last hours by a Salt Lake City doctor named Pendleton. He was grimly cheerful and kept asking her, "And do you feel any better now, Sister Dempsey?"

She was a true fact facer, my mother, and her answer summed up her life-long philosophy. "Dr. Pendleton," she replied, "you know very well I'm dying. If you ask me how I feel again I'll get out of this bed and punch you in the nose."

He didn't get another chance to inquire after her health. She died on that note of common sense and courage. They were her trademarks. She was two or three years shy of her ninetieth year.

I loved my mother.

My father sold three hundred acres of Logan County coal and timber for a dollar an acre, and with that fat sum, a prairie wagon, a wife and two kids he set off for the land of the Church of Jesus Christ of Latter-Day Saints. That would be about 1880.

Effie, my oldest sister, made the journey but couldn't remember it later on when the younger kids asked. Bernie couldn't remember the trip either, except that they stopped at Manassa, a Mormon settlement in the San Luis Valley some miles north of Alamosa, Colorado.

I believe Manassa was founded by a Mormon missionary named Hugh Sellers in 1878, so it was only just beginning when the Dempseys rolled in, broke and exhausted. It was a town of about a hundred then, almost all Mormons. All around Manassa was Mexican country. The towns had soft Spanish names, the people spoke only that tongue. Even today I can get by reasonably well in Spanish.

Manassa was a frontier town. One of the last. It lived off what it raised and grazed or hooked and shot. There was a little mining but too far away.

Florence and Stella were born there. They're gone now.

Joe was born next. He lives with me now, managing my apartment house. I don't know his age, because he won't tell me.

Then came Alice. Then Robert. Alice died before I was four and Robert before I was three. I remember neither of them. Then came poor, good-looking Johnny, who tried to be a fighter and couldn't make the grade and died by his own hand.

Johnny was only a year older than I. Elsie came after me. Bruce was the last, born in 1900. He was stabbed in the back while peddling newspapers in Salt Lake City when he was a teen-ager. Some crazy town half-wits, enraged by the taunts of other kids, chose my brother for this insane retaliation.

I was a pork-and-beans fighter around Seattle when Bruce was murdered. My mother wired me (she almost always knew where I was) and I rode the rods to my brother's funeral. And got there too late.

Bernie, the eldest, was the solid man of the Dempseys. He was a prize fighter for ten years and a good one. Blond, blue-eyed Dempsey. He had one incurable weakness in the ring, sadly enough. He had a chin of pure glass. But he could do everything else well. And he taught me my trade. Bernie owned a gym in Los Angeles when he died in 1935. He died of what we called "miners' tuberculosis," which I imagine is silicosis.

That's the Dempseys— eleven children, four living. There are uncountable children, grandchildren, and even great-grandchildren of those eleven around, mostly in the West.

The stronghold of the Dempsey clan remains in Logan

County. They're fine, hospitable people. There must be thousands of them. You go down there for a day and they want you to stay a month. I never had one ask me for a dime.

In 1957 I attended a gathering of the clan in Lenore, West Virginia. My lawyer telephoned me there from his New York office. He had a terrible time getting me. Twenty-six Jack Dempseys were ready to answer the call.

But back to the founders of the Western branch of the Dempseys in Manassa. My mother was having babies and Pop was working now and then, dreaming all the time of a better place and a better life.

I don't remember much about Manassa. But what I remember seems to tell the story of the Dempseys in Manassa.

We were never hungry. Mormons are never hungry. They keep close check on one another through the visits of Mormon "teachers." A "teacher" can be a doctor, a lawyer or a candlestick maker. Even a teacher. He drops in, casually, and asks how things are going. Polite and easy, without prying.

He reports back to the bishops on what he hears and sees. And if he has seen or sensed a bare cupboard it's filled before nightfall. Without comment.

If the poverty is because of a lazy father the man is summoned for a most thorough, frank dressing down. Whatever the effect of the lecture upon the father, neither he nor his family are ever without food. And warmth.

The Dempseys ate many a meal by grace of this silent, almost-but-not-quite-painless charity. And they ate and stayed warm that way in many a town long after Manassa was behind us.

I'm proud to be a Mormon. And ashamed to be the Jack Mormon I am.

The "teacher" and the big baskets of food are only two memories of Manassa.

We pulled our own teeth in Manassa. You don't forget that.

Bruce was born when I was about five. Dr. Friedenberg, the local horse-and-buggy practitioner, charged anywhere from twenty-five cents to a dollar for a visit, so you didn't call him unless you were dying. So Bruce was born as we all were, without doctor or midwife. And my mother almost died. There was a hemorrhage, I imagine. But even then we didn't call Dr. Friedenberg. Handled it as such things had to be handled on the frontier.

I remember the summer after Bruce was born we traveled an endless eighty-five miles by wagon to Creede, a mining town on the edge of the Great Divide. My mother had heard of a chance to make some money in Creede, so she took along those of us who were left (the young Dempseys died or departed early). She operated a boarding-house there for the summer. She took care of Joe, Johnny, Elsie, little Bruce and me. Also the old man. And took in washing on the side. That must have been when I started to know that my mother was a wonderful woman. And one of the unluckiest women alive.

There was a story my mother told me in Manassa. She

told it often there. And often through the years that followed.

"Just a little time before you were born," she would say, "a stranger came to the door. He was selling magazines. I told him I had no money for that sort of thing but he was welcome to come in and have a cool glass of milk. When he left he wanted to pay for the milk. I wouldn't hear of it, naturally. So he gave me a useless, battered old book he was toting. It was all about John L. Sullivan. I finished reading it just before you were born. I sure did enjoy it. When you were born, so big and strong, I said to everybody, 'William [it was to become Harry] is going to grow up to be the world's champion fighter. Just like John L. Sullivan.'"

Those are the memories of Manassa. I'm not sure when we left there. Counting back, I guess it must have been 1902. I was seven. I don't know why we left. Maybe my father's feet were itchy. The summer at Creede suggests serious financial troubles in Manassa. It was rugged in Manassa, I'm sure. But I'm equally certain we were never again as secure as we were there.

Our next "stop" was Uncompahgre, Colorado. It's 175 miles west across the Great Divide from Manassa. By prairie schooner, the way we traveled, it was supposed to take twelve to fourteen days. It took us two years.

We traveled a 600-mile route. Stopping and moving on. Living as we could for periods from a few weeks to a few months.

We stopped at Leadville. There was mining work or

railroad work for Joe or Johnny. Even for my father. We crossed the Great Divide and one of our two horses died from the climb.

My mother became desperately ill. She fainted frequently, was often dizzy and usually in pain. We turned around finally and got her back to Leadville. My father figured that the altitude was responsible for her ills and he decided it was wise to send her to my sister Florence, who now lived in Denver. Denver, to cure altitude sickness!

There was just enough money to buy a ticket for Mother to Denver. She refused to go without the baby, Bruce, Elsie, and little Harry — me.

With a ticket for herself, a dollar in change, two ticket-less half-fare children, and little Bruce in her arms, my mother set off. The conductor demanded tickets for Elsie and me. My mother said, "I'm very sick." That's all she said. Then she opened her purse and showed him the pitiful change it contained.

"Okay," he said after a while, "the girl can travel free. But that boy has to have a half-fare ticket or he gets thrown off at the next station."

No matter how poor you are you never get used to humiliation. I was humiliated. And terribly frightened that I would have to leave my mother.

A man across the aisle beckoned to me. I went over. He said, very low, "I don't think the conductor will bother you, kid. But tell your mother not to worry. If he insists on his money I'll pay it for you."

The conductor never bothered us. But I'll never forget the impression the incident made on me at that time. I got a sudden lust to be rich like the wonderful fellow across the aisle. So I would never be humiliated. Or frightened. In not too many years I added another adjective to "humiliated" and "frightened." It was "hungry."

My mother recovered quickly and completely in Denver. It wasn't the altitude at all. It was the exhaustion. But once she was herself again, we had to rejoin Pop. He had sold the last horse and wired us money to meet him in Wolcott. We stayed there a while. Then on to Steamboat Springs.

In Steamboat Springs I went to work. Hired out to a farmer with my father and brothers. I've never stopped working since— when I could get work. I was eight.

Then Mt. Harris for a while. Then six or seven months in Craig. Then Meeker. Then Rifle. And finally, in 1904, two years after we left Manassa, we really settled down in Delta, Colorado.

Mother had hated the huts and the crowded covered-wagon life. After our wandering like gypsies, my father's itchy feet were stilled. We settled in Delta for a short stay.

So it was on to Uncompahgre, near Montrose, Colorado. Our luck unaccountably changed. My father got a job as a rancher. A share rancher, actually. He worked a mile-square area called the Albrush Ranch. I started to get in my long-lost boyhood. I rode, I hunted, I fished. I was a real, honest-to-Injun working cowboy. We not only had a house, we had a two-story house. My mother was never without something to do, keeping us and the house and anyone who stopped by for a handout. The food was plentiful and varied, and she could really cook it.

We were happy and we worked hard, but we blew the ranch in a year. Joe, Johnny, Elsie, my mother and father and I did everything we could. But there's more to running a ranch than just sweating. That's where the boss, my father, came in. He just wasn't up to it.

We moved on to another ranch to sharecrop. It was the nearby Masters spread. How we worked to make that run! And we blew it in a year.

The railroad town of Montrose was twelve miles away. The Denver & Rio Grande was building the great Gunnison Tunnel. My mother figured the workers crowding into Montrose would have to eat. Hell, the Dempseys would have to eat too.

So she opened and operated a cheap hash house called the Rio Grande Eating House.

Harry, the proud cowboy, was now a dishwasher. I wasn't quite eleven. I would have been happy to punch cows forever. But washing dishes, waiting on table, serving tough railroad construction hands for two years made me a man.

So I guess I was a boy for only two years of my life.

Montrose was a big city as I knew such things. There was always something to do. Or to be done. None of it was much fun.

There was school. I had hated school at Uncompahgre because I was such a miserable student. But I had liked my classmates.

Not so at Montrose. In Montrose I was made aware each day that I was a "poor" kid, that I came from the wrong side of the tracks, that I wasn't really acceptable. In Uncompahgre I was dressed as my classmates were dressed. Ragged. In Montrose everybody dressed better than I did. It was tough.

There were chores too, and they seemed endless. First, there was the restaurant. Dishes to be washed, food to be served on the gallop, coal to be taken from the railroad yards each evening for the restaurant stove. And anything else to make a penny. Shoe shining. I peddled papers and the *Saturday Evening Post* and the *Ladies' Home Journal*.

And I started to learn my trade.

Bernie spent a lot of time in the mining camps. He was my idol. He was a prize fighter and he was a man. I think my adoration for the latter trait far exceeded any awe I felt for a fellow who lived by his fists. We'd been needing a man around the house for a long time.

Johnny was filled with ambition to be a fighter too. And anybody who watched Johnny and me working with Bernie would know at once that Johnny would be a fighter. Like Bernie, he was a good boxer and a fair hitter.

But neither Johnny nor the wonderful Bernie had one thing I always had. I loved to fight.

That's the word for it— "loved." There had been a thousand and one things I enjoyed doing through my life, but the two things I enjoyed most were fighting and mining. I know it's hard to believe, but I'm the only man I ever knew who actually enjoyed going into a mine to fight chunks of coal out of a wall. And the mines I worked in were the kind that required a man, or a kid— as I was— to work on his knees part of the day. I can't explain it, but I always felt wonderful deep in a mine.

And I always felt wonderful fighting. I don't think it was the thrill of competition. Hell, I had all the "competition" I ever needed in the job of existing, eating, from day to day. And I didn't enjoy fighting because I did it particularly well. In time, apparently, I did it somewhat better than fair. But in the beginning I was terrible. Have you ever loved something you were terrible at?

Bernie tried to teach me the classic moves. The feint, the jab, the counter and all the others he knew so well. I learned all these rudiments. Johnny learned them better.

Bernie was a good coach. His fragile chin told him I could hit. His eyes told him that my speed was out of the ordinary. I was a floundering, awkward greenhorn, but I could hit and I had fast hands. Bernie would come at me wagging a broom handle as fast as he could and yell at me to try to hit the stick with a jab or a punch. It wasn't easy, but lots of times I could.

So my own instinct and my brother's teaching combined to make speed my defense. My offense would be the punch I was born with.

Bernie had some special words of wisdom that paid off for me. He was painfully conscious of his china chin, so he insisted that I make my own jaw as hard as a rock. When I was eleven he had me chewing gum from pine trees, chewing the tough resinlike stuff all day long. It tastes awful.

At eleven I was also getting pails of beef brine from

butchers. Three times a day I bathed my face in the stinking liquid, to make it as tough as leather. Bernie had told me about fights being stopped because of simple face cuts, even though you might be winning.

In other words, at the age of eleven I was preparing to be a prize fighter. And, in the lean years to come, I chewed pine and bathed in brine even when I was a roving worker, or, if you want to call it that, a road bum. It was a habit that stayed with me a long time. Even when I was champion of the world, living in big homes, mingling with Hollywood movie stars, Broadway beauties or the big fellows of finance, I found time every day to chew pine and bathe in brine.

Now that my cow pony, my rifle, my hunting days were just memories, the only fun left was fighting. Whenever there was time I would fight. I lived to fight, just as later I would fight to live.

I fought Johnny, with Bernie watching closely. I don't think I ever put a glove to that handsome face Johnny protected so well. I wanted to punch it in, much as I liked him and looked up to him. I never lacked action.

In Montrose, big, sophisticated city that it was to me, but tough little railroad's Western outpost that it was in fact, there was always somebody to fight.

I suppose I had schoolboy fights, but I don't remember any. My Montrose fights were contests between friends after school. Like a golf match today. Or a tennis game at the country club. Instead of getting up a ball game, we'd clear a space and fight.

There were two families in Montrose much like the

Dempseys. There were the Woodses, white and poor, and the Pittses, black and even poorer. We were friends, so we fought and fought and fought. We stayed friends, although often bloody. There were a lot of Pittses and Woodses and Dempseys, so we paired off according to size. Fred Woods and Tommy Pitts were my size. Fred, Tommy and I all became professionals. Which we wanted like nothing else in the world— even at twelve.

The tunnel was finished and so was the Rio Grande Eating House. Time to move on once again. This time it was to Provo, in another state, Utah. Provo was forty miles from Salt Lake City and was much bigger than Montrose.

Provo wasn't too bad, even though there was school there. Wherever there was school I was usually in trouble. But this school had a track team and I learned I could run. Anything from the 50-yard dash to the 440. I did the 100 in ten seconds. We had a baseball team and a basketball team too, and my speed was enough to get me on both.

We stayed in Provo several years, leaving it only once. And that was a pretty fair jump. We retraced the journey my mother and father made in 1880. My father had been told— or decided himself— that he had 2,500 acres of Logan County timber-and-coal land due him under his father's will. So he pulled our roots in Provo and off we took. I seriously doubt that the journey west almost thirty years before had been any more uncomfortable.

Naturally, nothing came of the awful trip. I had a boy's crazy, hopeful dream that we'd all get rich when we got to Logan. But the land had been sold for taxes.

Whatever the reason, we were broke every minute in

Logan for months. I went into the mines. I'd work all one day drilling holes for powder. Then I'd blow the coal down. The next day I'd return and shovel away what had fallen.

Rough, dirty work. Most of it on my hands and knees. But I loved it. There was no law against child labor.

Logan was a rough, feuding, cockroach-poor mining town. It made even Provo, Utah, seem good by comparison. So the old man pulled his anchor again and took us all the way back across the country.

Provo was a Mormon town, and the land and the Mormon "teachers" made it a lot more attractive than Logan. We roamed around Provo like grazing animals, living first in one house and then in another and sometimes in a wagon. I lost track of the number of places we lived there, and I thought the memory of any one of those stops had left me forever.

But not long ago I had to go back to Provo on business. I'm a wandering good-will man for a national food store chain and often appear at openings of new stores. Now I was back in a town I had known as a kid, but except for seeing a few old friends like Clarence Johnson and Spencer Madison's wife I might just as well have been visiting Timbuktu. But then suddenly as I walked up to the store I was about to open I realized where I was. I was back in "the Bench," as they called that part of Provo where the flat valley starts to rise into the foothills.

I looked at the shiny new store, turned to Bill Slocum and said, "I lived right here on this spot once."

My mind went back nearly half a century to a skinny,

hungry kid everybody called Harry. It was 1910 again. Jim Jeffries had come out of retirement to fight Jack Johnson. The heavyweight championship had to be returned to the white race. I heard my father and my brothers talk about "white supremacy" and "white hope" by the hour. I hung a homemade punching bag in an old chicken house behind our house. I drew two faces on the big bag. One face was that of a white man. The other was a Negro. Chalk and charcoal were my paints.

When Johnson won we were all stunned. I rubbed out the chalk face and replaced it with one done in charcoal. So I had a black face to punch no matter how the bag twisted. That's how seriously we took things in those days.

I thought more of punching away at those two black faces on my bag than anything else, including, of course, school. The presence of wonderful old Brigham Young University in Provo meant nothing to me as a kid, I'm not proud now to say. I was a real bum scholar. I remember my Lakeview School teacher, George Wintz, saying to me, at about the time I was swinging away at my punching bag every chance I had, "Harry Dempsey, you're the oldest boy in this grade school and the dumbest. You'll never amount to a thing."

In Provo, around 1910, I worked at anything that came along. I had learned to shine shoes earlier in Montrose, and I tried that again in Provo. I went to the fields and picked whatever was in season. The town had a beet refinery, and when the beets came in I worked at emptying the railroad cars that brought them.

I'd climb a mountain of beets and start pitching the big,

basketball-sized vegetables off the cars. Without realizing it, I was building muscles and perfecting my footwork. The footing was unsteady. I had to crouch by the hour, changing my position in a hurry every now and then or I would fall on my face. That same crouch was perhaps the most important weapon I owned later in the ring. I liked unloading beets. The money was good— a dime a ton. In a good long day I could unload ten to fifteen tons.

There were mines nearby, too. I worked them, at from ten to fifteen cents a ton. Matter of fact, I worked wherever I could at whatever I could. I quit only one job in my life. One day, while shining shoes and cleaning up a Provo barbershop, I heard that there was going to be a bicycle race from Provo to Salt Lake City the following Saturday. I asked the boss for that day off, so I could enter and maybe win a few bucks. He wouldn't give me the time off, so I quit. It was a mistake. I pedaled forty miles through a desert that was like a furnace and finished so far back that they weren't counting any more.

But there was some fun in Provo, too. Saturday nights there were girls to be walked or taken to a magic-lantern show. There were dances every other week. I couldn't dance a lick, but I enjoyed going to them very much. They always ended with a midnight supper— canned oysters, pie and a lot of other good things to eat.

It was not like some Colorado towns where, when the food was gone, the older guys started drinking. The fights would start about one o'clock in the morning, just like clockwork. I'd grab a ringside seat, if they weren't using the chair on each other, and study the styles. I learned a lot of things not to do, watching those drunks brawl.

Reading schoolbooks was torture for me, but I found to my surprise that reading something else was easier. The something else was the *Police Gazette,* the favorite reading matter at the barbershop. When a new issue came in, I'd take the old one home and cut out the pictures I liked— mostly fighters and dogs. The favorite I pinned on my wall was a Bob Edgren cartoon of Bob Fitzsimmons, a skinny old guy covered with a lot of funny-looking dots. His record impressed me more than any other heavy-weight's. Fitz was my kind of a fighter, a one-punch guy. He could take anybody out with a single shot, I believed, and I wanted to do the same thing.

It was hard waiting to be old enough and big enough, but there were plenty of things to occupy the time. Working to help the family get along, for instance. When I couldn't find work, I fished in Lake Utah, to help fill our supper table. Or I hunted and trapped, not for fun but for food or profit.

And then, suddenly, there was more time for everything I wanted to do. In the middle of June 1911, just a few days shy of my sixteenth birthday, Mr. Wintz knew he was over-matched. He let me graduate from Lakeview School.

I got out of town.

CHAPTER **3**

>> <<

I WAS AN AWFUL LOT OF THINGS BE-
tween the ages of sixteen and nineteen, but a bum wasn't
one of them. I don't think I was ever a bum. I lived in hobo
jungles. I begged for work and food. I rode the rods because I didn't have the loose change to ride the freights,
and, of course, I didn't have the important money you
needed if you wanted to ride on a ticket.

» 30 «

There's quite a difference between riding the rods and bumming it in freight trains. Most bums aren't steady enough to ride the rods, the two narrow steel beams beneath a Pullman. There's only a few inches between you and the tracks and roadbeds— and death. If you fall asleep you'll roll off your narrow steel bed and die. If you're so cold you can't hold on any longer, you die. You can't ride too long without rest if it's rods you're riding on. But there aren't any bells to ring to tell the man "Stop, kind sir, I want to get off." You don't know how long it will be between stops. On warm nights you don't worry too much about that. But on winter nights in the mountain states, well, I often bet my life that the train would stop and let me off before I shook and shivered my way to my death beneath the wheels. You have to be desperate to gamble like that, but if you weren't desperate you wouldn't be on the rods.

If you had a few cents— a dime, a quarter, half a buck, let's say— you could ride upstairs, in the luxury of maybe a freezing freight car. It always cost, unless you could show a union card. In those days, a union card entitled any man to ride free in a freight car. The conductors, brakemen and railroad dicks who patrolled the freights always asked the same question of the bums they found free-loading: "What're you riding on— card or money?" If no card could be shown, the bum had to turn his money over to the railroad people, or get kicked off. Most of them would give up what they had and ride in peace until a new crew came on and repeated the shakedown.

Many of the men riding freights were workers moving

from one job to another as cheaply as possible. Others were just tramps— bindle stiffs. I was never a bindle stiff, though I shared many a jungle meal with these strange guys who wandered the country with their wardrobe and fortune tied in a rag, or bindle.

They weren't a bad bunch, really. You were always free to walk into any of their jungles and dip into the Mulligan stew simmering over a fire. There was only one rule: You had to throw something reasonably edible into the stew-pot, or can. One wormy potato was enough.

Sometimes you'd run into a kindhearted railroad fellow and he'd take a chance and give you a break, let you ride without shaking you down. And sometimes you'd run into guys so cruel you wanted to kill them.

I hopped a freight moving out of Grand Junction, Colorado, one cold afternoon, right after running away from home. I was headed for Delta, forty miles away. I had just grabbed the ladder when a railroad man on top of the freight spotted me. He had a long broomstick in his hand, like a cop's billy. He yelled at me to jump off. I couldn't. The train had picked up too much speed. So, very systematically, and while the train picked up more speed, he kept belting me with that club and split open my head. I jumped or fell off, crashing face down in the cinders along the way. I thought I'd never stop rolling.

I walked the forty miles to Delta while the blood dried.

That's how I moved in those days. I moved because moving was part of the business of survival. When all the peaches had been picked in one town, we'd hear that the beets were coming in a hundred miles away. I'd move. Or word might seep down that somebody was running fight cards in Utah or over in Nevada. I'd move. Or the sheriff might drop a gentle hint. Something like "Get outa here, bum." I'd move.

I always considered myself a professional prize fighter in those days after my graduation from the eighth grade. But it was sometimes a long wait between fights. Even if I got a fight, the pickings were slim, and my managers would see that they got even slimmer.

Who knows how many fights I had between 1911 and 1916? The record books don't contain them, and I couldn't name the number or identify all the faces today if my life depended on doing it. I'd guess a hundred. But that's still a guess. Whatever the number was, it wasn't enough to support me. To fill the gaps, and my belly, I was a dishwasher, a miner of anything you could dig up in Nevada, Utah, Colorado and Idaho— I dug ditches, potatoes and beets— punched cattle, shined shoes, and was a porter in the Hotel Utah in Salt Lake City.

When there was nobody to fight, and nothing to dig or to pick from trees or to unload from railroad cars, I went to the back door of the best-looking house I could find in a town. I didn't beg. I always said the same thing. I said, "Lady, have you got any chores a fellow could do in exchange for a meal? Or a few cents."

I washed windows, cut lawns or firewood, scrubbed floors. I made millions of bucks later, but at that time one buck was a fortune. Sometimes a door was slammed in my face, which figures. But people generally were pretty nice. If there was work for me, I worked as hard as I could.

When there was no work, there were handouts lots of times. I'd rather go hungry for days than steal.

No matter what has been written, I was never a bum. I bummed for jobs. I never turned down a job anybody offered me, no matter what the pay.

There's something else I never was too, though it has been written a thousand times. I never was a saloon bouncer. Maybe the story came out of the fact that I lived in, and off, saloons for pretty nearly six years. I fought in saloons. I couldn't guess how many fights I had in saloons.

When things were real tough I'd walk into a strange saloon and say, like a skinny John L. Sullivan, "I can lick anybody in the house." Unlike John L., who had a lot of class, I guess, I'd add, "For a buck." I weighed 130. That helped. It got me a lot of fights. Some of the guys who took me on weighed a hundred pounds more than I did. But as it turned out I murdered most of them.

As time went on I found an even better way of making money fighting in saloons. In this dodge, I worked with the bartender. I usually met the bartender real quick in a strange saloon. Chances were that after he watched me for a bit at the free-lunch counter he'd yell, "All right, bum, you've eaten ten bucks' worth of food for that lousy nickel beer you bought. Don't you think you oughta buy another?

I usually didn't have enough to buy another. So I'd talk to the fellow and make him a proposition. It was always this: If he'd be the matchmaker he could have a cut of the dough from passing the hat after I fought somebody.

"We get enough fights in here without arranging none," the guy would usually growl at me.

That was what I wanted to hear. I'd look at him and say, "You know, I'll bet you got some guy hanging around here who annoys you and your good customers, and nobody wants to take him on."

It almost never failed. There was bound to be at least one real bully in every Western saloon, a pain in the neck to everybody from the owner to the lowest customer. Everybody always wanted to see the bum flattened— and would pay to see it, which was more important.

The thought of having a social problem solved at personal profit always interested a bartender. Sometimes the guy wouldn't think much of my chances after looking me over, but the fact that somebody actually wanted to fight a bum who had given him a lot of headaches, and split the profits from the hat collection, was almost too good to be true. He couldn't wait for the pest to come in that night, and to sick me on him. Or just the other way around.

The guy always was looking for a fight when he came in. Sometimes I started the conversation, sometimes he did. Sometimes the bartender would give me a loud build-up. But one thing was always the same: I looked and sounded like something the tough guy could have eaten for breakfast. Sure, by today's standards I probably looked real tough— broken nose, maybe a sweater instead of a shirt, boots, half-shaven head, a few scars. But *everybody* looked tough in a Western saloon.

What made all those guys willing and ready to fight me was, first, my weight, and, second, the fact I was obviously still a kid. But the clincher always came when they heard me talk.

I sounded like a girl.

I didn't hit like a girl, though. Some of those tough guys fought like mountain lions. Some couldn't have licked my sister. It didn't matter to me. I took all of them out, and I took them out as quick as I could. I learned early that it's dangerous to "carry" a 200-pound copper miner, let's say. My motto became "The sooner the safer."

It remained my motto as a preliminary boy, then a cheap main-event fellow and through the days of the million-dollar gates. The one time I tried to coast with a fighter, to make it look good, I came very close to being flattened. I'll tell you about that later.

When the tough guys of the Western saloons were finally on their backs, or lying there on the floor with their faces in the sawdust, the hat would be passed. Sometimes, depending on how much the people hated the bum, I'd get as much as fifty dollars. The bartender usually would take half. I'd mail a five- or ten-spot to my mother in Provo. With the rest, I'd have a few beers (I was never much of a drinker but I knew what the stuff tasted like), a real meal and maybe a date with a girl.

Then I'd have to look around for a new saloon, a new guy to flatten, or peaches to pick, something to dig, a cheap fight club, a back door, or the rods.

I began making Salt Lake City my base and fanning out from there. Today, of course, it's a model city, highly moral and quiet.

It was the heart of Mormonism, sure. But the Mormons didn't control the city then as they do today. The "Gentiles" had power through what was called the American Party. The American Party and the Mormons were enemies. Finally they had a big compromise meeting between the leaders. The gist of it was that the "Gentiles" could have the area around Commercial Street for whatever sinning they wanted to do.

I guess Commercial Street was one of the best-named streets we ever had. Everything went on Commercial Street, probably because it couldn't go anywhere else in Salt Lake City. If the "Gentiles" tried anything beyond Commercial Street, things were made tough for them. The Mormons, of course, always behaved. If they didn't, they were thrown out of the church.

Commercial Street nearly got me down. I guess I came as close to being a bum there as I ever came. For example, I learned to shoot pool, shoot it well enough to be one of the street's best pool hustlers. I bowled real good too. In fact, I bowled a lot better after the bets were placed than I did before. That's the definition of a pool or bowling hustler. Play like a bum until the cash is up. I'd take on any player in the house for a buck. Or find a new bar with a new pest and fight him for half the collection. Or fight with gloves in a real ring, for peanuts.

I spent some time with girls, along Commercial Street. They were, let's say, named for the street. We got along well.

Why didn't I look around for the sweet girl graduate? Well, I owned a shirt, a sweater, a pair of pants, a pair of beat-up shoes or boots, and no future.

With such clothes and manners it was a cinch I wasn't going to be asked up to dinner by the daughter of a bishop, or even a hardware store keeper. I liked them for

DEMPSEY *by the Man Himself*

companionship, for laughs, comfort, somebody to tell your troubles to.

My chief hangout in Salt Lake City became a saloon-gym run by an old fighter from the East, young Peter Jackson (not *the* Peter Jackson). I hustled pool there, I'm sorry to admit. But I also earned an honest buck as a rubber of fighters in training. I'd drop in there for any kind of work I could find, after a hard day as a porter at the Utah Hotel.

It was at Jackson's that I won the most embarrassing fight of my life. I was playing a little pea pool with a fellow for twenty-five cents, and we got into an argument over something that's been long since forgotten. I flattened him with one punch. He fell over like a tree, and no wonder. He had a wooden leg. I walked out after the punch and didn't learn for a few days that I had hit a cripple. I'll never get over the sight of seeing him on crutches while he waited for the new leg I helped him buy.

Jackson's wasn't Sunday school. I got into a fight with a customer one night, a no-pay fight, and he knew everything I knew and maybe more. We stood in front of the bar and slugged it out for a good fifteen minutes before I nailed him and then he quit. I took a cigar and walked to the gas cigar lighter— strutting, I guess— and stuck my stogie into the flame.

"Look out!" somebody yelled, and just as the yell reached my ears I ducked. It was my recent opponent, hurling a beer stein at me. He missed. For nothing. Today, on television, it would be considered one of the fights of the century.

I fought as a pro too, with gloves, in Salt Lake City in those days. A promoter named Hardy Downey put on a show every Monday night. Over the years, Hardy promoted maybe six thousand fights and he got more or less rich off them because he always made his fighters fight.

Little Hardy was his own referee. If a fighter dogged it, Hardy would stop the bout and throw the guy who wasn't fighting out of the ring. He'd yell, as the poor bum walked down the aisle, "And don't bother stopping at the box office. There ain't nothin' there for you."

So 'most everybody fought real good for Downey. We all knew that he meant every word of his "No fight, no dough" policy. It's a policy that would solve a lot of the problems of modern-day fighting, I think.

I made my official Salt Lake City debut for Hardy. The purse was $2.50. My opponent was One-Punch Hancock. We touched gloves for fifteen seconds, and then I took One-Punch with one punch.

I was pretty pleased with this, but Hardy wasn't. "I didn't get much of a run for my money, kid," he said. "Let's see if I can get you another."

I needed another $2.50, so I said sure. Hardy hung over the ropes and bawled, "Kid Blackie here (that was the name I had around the saloons) wants to know if anybody else wants to fight him."

"I sure do," a guy at ringside roared, ripping off his shirt. "He's a lucky little bum." He climbed into the ring like a storm. He was big.

"And who might you be?" Hardy asked him.

The guy pointed to One-Punch, sitting on his stool in

his corner, still out like a light. "I'm his brother," he said. He couldn't wait to get the gloves on.

I flattened him in twenty seconds.

Hardy paid me five dollars for the two fights. I walked away on air. Just think, I kept saying to myself, five whole bucks for only thirty-five seconds of fighting! I felt I was on my way at last.

But I was to earn less, and many times, before I earned a lot more.

CHAPTER **4**

THE MONEY AT HARDY DOWNEY'S GOT
a little better, and so did the competition. I'd make as
much as twenty dollars at times. I won usually, but certainly not always. And I learned a little more every time
I went against one of those older fellows. Or even against
young toughs like myself.

At seventeen I had a pretty good understanding of what I could do and what I couldn't. I was a preliminary fighter, no boxer but a pretty good hitter and hard to tag. To make myself harder to hit, I kept working on the crouch.

It's an exhausting way to fight, that crouch. I'd practice shadowboxing in that position for eight or ten rounds. I even built a kind of low-ceiling cage once, the size of a ring but only three or four feet high. I spent hours in it, ducking the ceiling, throwing punches. And I never missed chewing the pine sap gum and washing my face in brine, when I could get it. I always enjoyed training, whether it was for peanuts or, as it turned out later on, a fortune.

I was a lousy student in school but I never missed studying an opponent. I'd look for his goods and his bads. I'd find out in a hurry whether he was a puncher or a boxer, whether his chin or his belly was tough. I learned as a kid that no fighter has everything. If his chin is pure concrete, the belly may be jelly. And just the reverse. If he boxes well, he probably can't punch. If he has a great punch, he probably can't box.

In those early fights, if it was a boxer I was against I'd take everything he had, on my brine-soaked face, while I got set to nail him. If he was a hitter who could hurt me, my crouch and speed were my defense. I'd wait. There was no sense slugging with a slugger who outweighed me maybe fifty or a hundred pounds until I was pretty certain I had a real good shot at him, a shot that would do a lot of damage. It didn't take much intelligence to learn these things. Hit a fellow on the chin, and if he doesn't blink hit him in the belly. Simple as that. And if he hits you a lick and hurts you, keep away from that hand that did the damage. Nobody hits equally hard with both hands.

I always wanted to know everything possible about the fellow I was signed to fight. In the early days I had to learn by getting a punch on the chin. Years later, Kearns would drive me daffy by saying, over and over again, "You'll knock him dead in the first heat, Jack." "Yeah," I'd say, "if he don't knock me dead first." Then I'd usually say, "Find out something about this guy, Jack, I'd like to know."

That's not asking too much of a manager. Leo Flynn was a manager who understood this. Leo knocked out Jack Sharkey for me, just by going out and finding out something about him. But I must say that Kearns always got me the best sparring partners he could find. They were always good, tough, expensive fighters who fought in the style of my next opponent and got me ready for almost anything that might come.

Maybe you think I've gone overboard on this particular point, but I haven't. I think this refusal to take anything for granted made me heavyweight champion.

Smart as I was, or as I think I was, it was still tough for me to raise a buck during those days in Salt Lake City. There just weren't enough fights, or, to put it another way, enough fighters who wanted to fight me.

I got a couple of fights in Montrose by promoting them myself. I made twenty-five cents the price of a ticket, which gives you some idea of the kind of gates they drew. At Montrose Freddy Woods and I announced we were a promoting team. For a while we looked around for somebody to fight for us, but it was hopeless. So we fought each other.

It was a beaut of a fight. I barely got back to my corner after the second round. We went after each other like lifelong enemies until the seventh, and then I knocked him out.

We split eighty dollars and together had a few beers.

A small-time promoter from Durango saw the fight and offered me a bout with an old middleweight named Andy Malloy. It was one of the best breaks of my life, as it turned out. Andy was thirty. I was eighteen. He had forgotten more about fighting than I knew.

Among the fighters he had beaten over the years was my brother Bernie.

(Bernie always fought under the name of "Jack" Dempsey. Any fighter whose name was Dempsey wanted to be called "Jack," because it made him sound as tough and as good as the original Jack Dempsey, who was always called Jack Dempsey the Nonpareil. He was middleweight champ for years, toward the end of the last century. My brother Johnny also fought under the name of Jack Dempsey, which was fair enough. Anyway, I thought there might be too many Jack Dempseys around, so I used Harry Dempsey or Kid Blackie.)

As Kid Blackie, I fought Malloy ten rounds in Durango. I got thirty dollars for that fight. I also got a first-class licking, and I made a friend— Malloy.

He was a fine man, Malloy, a fellow who had fought a long time for peanuts. After beating me he came to my so-called dressing room and said, "Kid, you've got something. Why don't you let me manage you?"

"Sure," I said.

Malloy got me a fight at once, in Moose Hall, Montrose. I felt he had overmatched me. He put me in there against himself.

I flattened my manager in three heats. When Andy regained consciousness and remembered where he was, he seemed happy that I had flattened him. He said it proved he was a good judge of fighters. It proved something to me, too— my ability to learn something by mixing previously with a man I was going to fight.

Malloy just couldn't get me a fight for some time after that. Both of us griped about that, but actually it was a good thing. We filled in the time by studying boxing. Bernie came around to help Andy work on me. They were both great teachers. I was an awful lucky kid to have them.

Still, Malloy and I split. There wasn't any difference of opinion. It was just discouragement.

He booked me into Olathe, Colorado, to fight some guy named Ed Something-or-other. He was a fighter-rassler, but the understanding was that we'd box. It was going to be on a winner-take-all basis.

Malloy and I checked into a $5-a-week room in an Olathe boardinghouse. I couldn't wait for the fight to start. Andy had taught me so many new moves that I couldn't wait to try them out. But I never got to. At least on Ed Whatever-his-name-was.

I was dressing for the fight when the sheriff walked in. I guess he must have been related to Ed.

"We don't permit fighting in this town," he said. "You've got to rassle Ed."

"*You* rassle him," I said. "I can't rassle."

"There's a lot of people out there, all come to see a rassling match," the sheriff said, like a cop about to give you a ticket.

"Well, that's tough," I said. "I came here to fight, not rassle. I'd get killed by a rassler." I turned to Andy. "Let's get out of here."

The sheriff sucked his teeth, then looked at the ceiling. "You're the boss," he said to me. "Go right ahead. But, by the way, your landlady tells me you owe her five bucks rent you should have paid in advance. Unless you pay her, I'm gonna throw you in jail. We've got a law here about paying rent, too, just like we got a law saying no fighting."

So I rassled Ed. I took a brutal going-over. He threw me twice in less than five minutes. I could have belted him out with a punch, but most of the time he was choking me or tying my skinny arms and legs in knots.

We got a big fat nothing for that night's work. We wandered around town, broke, and got to the railroad yards just as the sun was coming up. Malloy had a girl he was in love with, back in Montana. I had nothing. It seemed a good enough time to go our own ways. There were two trains ready to pull out. The last I saw of Andy Malloy he was standing on the roof of a northbound freight. I was on top of a southbound boxcar, headed for Salt Lake City.

We waved.

Back in Salt Lake City I got a fight for $2.50 against a local boy named Jack Downing. He beat me in four rounds. I fought him again for ten dollars and was boxing rings around him when he dropped me with a real good shot to the jaw near the end of the fourth. I just made it up on my feet when the bell sounded, ending the fight. I didn't know where I was, but I was given a draw.

I guess I should have been happy, but I wasn't. If the positions had been reversed I'd have been sore as hell. Downing should have been given that fight. Sure, I made him look like a bum for almost the entire fight. But fighting is something you do to find out who's the better man. The man in better shape at the end of four or forty rounds is the better man. Downing was in better shape than I was, so I think he was robbed. And lots of others have been robbed the same way through ring history.

We fought again, and I stiffened him in two. A fellow learns as he goes along.

As usual, now that I thought I was on my way in the fight game nobody wanted to fight me. At least nobody around Salt Lake City. So I climbed back on the rods and didn't care where the train took me.

It took me to Reno. I got a meal in a jungle, headed into town and cased the saloons and the gyms, and pretty soon I had the promise of a fight with a good but real cozy fighter named Anamas Campbell, a guy about the size and color of Jack Johnson. Still, he wouldn't close the deal until he had a chance to box six or eight rounds with me in a gym. I was always a rotten gym fighter, but this time I made sure I looked bad. He gave me a good lacing.

When the money was up, I hit him on the chin and knocked him out in the first round. In those days, there was a theory that Negro fighters couldn't take it in the stomach but had chins of iron. But I had learned in our gym workout that he had a good belly. So I went for the jaw and it worked.

When Anamas came to, he shook hands with me, grinned a big white-toothed grin and said to the people around us in the ring, "I knew this white boy was kiddin' me in the gym. Should never have fought him."

Everybody else around Reno figured they "should never have fought him," too. I went back on the rods and worked the mines and orchards again, to eat. But that fall— it was 1914— I heard from home that Bernie was going to fight in Cripple Creek, Colorado, though he was pushing forty. They had given my brother no soft touch, either. They had him in there against George Copelin, who could hit and box. I hit the rods for Cripple Creek, to see if I could help. As it turned out, I did.

I was helping Bernie get ready for his fight when he suddenly said, "Harry, I feel terrible. It's the altitude, I think. I don't want to fight this guy."

"Aw, come on, Bernie, anybody can flatten him," I told him. I guess it didn't sound very kind.

He looked at me and then said, "Then you flatten him."

We finally talked the promoter into making the switch, but he had a tough time selling the idea to the crowd and Copelin. The Club, the dive where the fight was held, almost collapsed from the boos. The fans knew I wasn't the real Jack Dempsey. It had seen Bernie fight before and knew that a phony was being palmed off on it. I weighed 150, Copelin around 165.

"I might kill that skinny guy," Copelin said to the promoter, worried.

"Listen," I said to the promoter, "I'll flatten this big bum. You can go out and bet my end on it." That convinced him. He introduced the fight, trying to make himself heard above the yells.

It was the first time I was introduced as Jack Dempsey, and they booed the hell out of me.

I dumped Copelin as soon as I could reach him. He got up immediately. I dropped him again. And again. Easily six times in the first round. And twice in the second. He was easy, as I had told my brother. But in the third round I started having trouble breathing. The altitude was beginning to do more to me than Copelin could. He didn't mind it a bit. The weaker I got, the stronger he got. At the end of six, I fell on the stool and said to Bernie, "I'm through. I quit."

Now it was Bernie's time to work on me, as I had tried to work on him earlier. As he gave me the water and wiped off the blood he said, "He's in worse shape than you are. He's gotta go this round."

I staggered out there and knocked Copelin down again. He got up. A minute later I floored him again. It took everything I had left to belt him down. I had trouble standing up and I said to myself, "If he gets up, I'm going to quit. Right in front of everybody. Even Bernie."

Copelin got up.

It was just too much. But I guess he must have been on the edge of death, because before I could quit and stagger out of the ring the referee grabbed him and stopped the fight. That was unusual. In those days they didn't stop mining-town fights as long as one guy could move.

The Copelin fight was one of the worst experiences of my life. But the thought of collecting the hundred dollars Bernie had been guaranteed helped me forget the pain and exhaustion. I stumbled into the dressing room. Every breath I took was like swallowing hot lead. The promoter came in with a fistful of money and a lot of congratulations and paid me the $100.

Bernie and I didn't bother cutting up the $100. We just paid what we owed in Victor. Bernie went back to the mines. I hit the road. There was a ten-dollar fight here, a double sawbuck there, an orchard or a mine somewhere else, or saloon fights in Reno. Lots of times it was a knock on the door, back door mostly, and a "Pardon me, ma'am, but do you have any chores a fellow can do?"

It was during this period that I had my first fight with Johnny Sudenberg and got carried home in a wheelbarrow. Even getting that fight was tough. I had to qualify for it. Goodfriend, the promoter, put me in a gym in the back of a saloon to see how I could do against a smart old Negro named Slick Merrill. The combination of hunger, some recent days on the rods and Slick's good left hand had me reeling all over the place.

"You look lousy," Goodfriend said from ringside, chewing a cigar.

Slick charged me, looking to knock me out. I fell into

a clinch, openmouthed, and accidentally bit a chunk out of his forehead. Blood poured down his face like a waterfall. Goodfriend signed me for the Sudenberg fight. Maybe he figured that if I couldn't fight I could at least bite.

We were rematched for Tonopah a month later, despite the awful beating he gave me in the first fight. I lived through that month by washing dishes and getting free lunches in the saloons.

I got to Johnny very fast in the Tonopah fight. He was down a number of times in the first round. But he was tough and smart. He covered and made me chase him for the next five. By the sixth, that free-lunch training table started to tell on me. He stretched me out three times in the seventh. For the rest of the fight we just stood there and hit each other until we couldn't hold our hands up. It was called a draw, and I think that's just what it was.

We collected a hundred dollars each for that massacre in the sun. We patched up our cuts and with money in our pockets found the nearest bar and walked in arm in arm. Everybody yelled hurray. The bartender set us up some cold beer and wouldn't take our money.

But two other guys would.

Suddenly there was a strange silence in the joint. The bartender put up his hands. Johnny and I turned around. Two tough-looking guys had guns on us. They cleaned us and the others. Completely. I was broke again.

Johnny and I gathered our few belongings and walked to the edge of town. We saw a handcar sitting there on the tracks, with nobody watching it. We took it.

Johnny and I hand-pumped that heavy car all the way

to a town called Miner Junction. I don't remember how far it was, but when we got there we were completely pooped, punchy and starving. We found a saloon.

"We're prize fighters," Johnny said out loud as we came into the place. "We'll fight ten rounds for you right now if you'll let us pass the hat."

We fought our bloody best for ten rounds and passed the hat. They had chipped in $3.60. We had fought thirty awful minutes for a buck-eighty each. I could have begged that much in an hour. Sometimes you can get a lot more on your knees than you can on your feet.

Johnny and I beat our way to Reno. Our luck changed. Word of our fights up in the hills had reached Reno and we were matched for $150 each.

It seemed too good to be true, and it was. Johnny didn't show. Nobody else would box me. So I didn't get a nickel. I never knew why he ducked. He was a decent guy and he sure wasn't afraid of me. That I know from thirty rounds of trying to scare him.

An ex-fighter named Roy Moore— a fellow I had sparred with while training for this fight that never came off— tried to cheer me up when it became certain there wouldn't be any substitute for Sudenberg.

"Aw, to hell with it, Jack. Let's go fishing," he said. There wasn't anything else to do so I said okay and we started out. Down by the railroad station Roy said, "We need some hooks, Jack. Hold my dog while I buy some."

I stood there holding the dog's leash, thinking of what a hell of a day it had been for me, and what a hell of a life. A train was picking up speed right in front of me. I tied Roy's mutt to a pole and in seconds I was back on the road again. Couple days later I rolled out from under a train in Salt Lake City, broke, filthy, and disgusted with Jack Dempsey, the so-called prize fighter.

I was ready to give up. I got a job where I figured I really belonged— with a ditchdigging gang. Buck-sixty a day. At least I'd eat regularly. And I'd be able to get over to Provo now and then to see my mother.

But pretty soon I was hanging around Jackson's saloon-gym again and going to the fights. I wanted to stay away, but I just couldn't. Then I met a Salt Lake City boy named Jack Price. He wanted to manage me. I told him to go right ahead. Price had the usual trouble trying to get me a fight in the town, but one day he came up with something real interesting.

There was a colored fighter who called himself the Boston Bearcat doing well around Ogden, Utah. Bearcat had come from the East, claiming he had stayed twenty rounds with Sam Langford. He belted out what there was around Ogden, then ran into the same trouble I was finding. So they matched a couple of guys nobody else wanted to fight.

He was a big sucker, full-sized heavyweight. I weighed 160, give or take a couple. I went into my crouch right at the start, and he looked twice as big as I did. I looked up and saw his belly and I dug a punch in there that went in as far as my wrist. Bearcat went down and out.

That quick kayo got me another fight in Ogden. This time it was Terry Keller, a local boy. I won the decision. Then a fight with a fellow who was pretty well known through the West, Bob York. I nailed him in the fourth.

Then nothing. I had run out of opponents again. But just when it looked like it was going to be permanent, I got a fight that helped change my life.

Joe Bond, a fighter out of Tacoma, Washington, had had a good tour of Australia and now, in the spring of 1916, was working his way through the West picking up some easy money. Jack Price signed me to fight him in Ely, Nevada. I had read about Bond. He was far and away the best man I had signed to face up to that time.

I don't think he had read anything about me. When I was introduced to him before the fight in Ely he gave me a filthy look. He was so confident it was embarrassing.

Anyway, what happened in Ely eventually brought Jack Kearns and me together. Kearns had been Bond's manager. They had busted up before the Ely fight for reasons I never knew.

I licked Kearns's ex-meal ticket real good. Bond could take a punch well, and he boxed so well that it was almost impossible to hit him two good shots in a row. But I had learned my trade pretty well too by now. There was no question about who won the fight.

It was a win fit to make a young fighter's head swim, and his manager's, too. Price and I rode to Salt Lake City.

The glow lasted for some time. One night we were sitting in a Salt Lake City bar. He was telling me how good I was, and I wasn't giving him any argument at all. The more he talked, the more he gave me an idea

"Jack," I asked him, "you got any money?"

That's one way to lose a manager. But after a while Price said, "Yeah. I got a little over two hundred."

"So have I," I said. "Let's go to New York and make some real money."

"New York!" he said, like it was China. "Are you crazy, Harry? They got *real* fighters there."

"I'm a real fighter," I said.

Price thought it over. Then he said, "Okay— but I won't ride them damned rods with you another foot."

"Forget it, kid," I said, lighting up a cigar and eying the girl at the piano to see if she was impressed. "Forget it. We'll ride the plush. We'll just fight our way east. Stop off at a town, flatten some bum, jump a couple hundred miles, do the same thing, and keep going until we hit New York."

We shook on it. Then I walked over to talk to the girl at the piano. Girl named Maxine. She'll be back in this story. Indeed she will.

The next day I had the pleasant experience of buying a railroad ticket. It was the first time I had ever done anything like that in my life. I felt a little guilty. I was headed for the big time.

CHAPTER 5

NOBODY THREW ANY TICKER TAPE THE
day I got to New York. It was a hot June morning, 1916.
Price and I arrived sharing an upper berth.

The trip east from Salt Lake City hadn't panned out as I
had hoped. We did stop off at the big cities— Kansas City,
St. Louis, Chicago, Cleveland— and we enjoyed the sights

and what the joints had to offer, but I just couldn't get a fight. It was hard to believe at first, but nobody had ever heard of Jack Dempsey, the Salt Lake Tiger. We'd show the promoters a little clipping I had, about beating Joe Bond, and most of them asked, "Who the hell is Joe Bond?" We'd tell them about how I flattened the Boston Bearcat in one round, the man who went twenty rounds with the great Sam Langford. And they'd say, "Never heard of him. Probably a phony." A four-round preliminary was the only work I got during the six weeks it took us to reach New York.

I was skinny, beetle-browed, needed a shave every four hours, had a broken nose, no clothes, and was scared stiff. I talked with a Western accent, but it wasn't one of those manly drawls like the deputies on TV. I talked soprano, and real fast. My grammar was brutal. I must have set a new record for greenhorns. The first night I got to Forty-second and Broadway I asked a man where I could find the "Great White Way" I had heard so much about. He burst out laughing at me.

That first morning, Price and I walked across town from Grand Central to Sixth Avenue, carrying our cardboard suitcases and looking for a bar that wouldn't throw us out. Finally we took a chance on one and got the information we needed. The best place to find fights was around Grupp's Gym on 116th Street. Price hustled a cheap room for us near the Polo Grounds.

Our Salt Lake suits were right out of a window on Commercial Street, but we figured it would help if we kept them neat and pressed. Price and I were the same size.

When my suit needed pressing, I'd wear his to the tailor shop while he stayed home in his drawers. And vice versa.

But regular pressing soon disappeared, and so did regular eating. It was just about the loneliest time of my life. New York was so damned big. Nobody gave a damn about me. After people started laughing at my voice and the fast way I talked, I began being afraid to open my mouth. The only places where I was comfortable were our room and Grupp's.

I wasn't impressive, ever, in the ring at Grupp's. But there was some comfort in seeing a lot of other hungry young guys, just as poor as I was, and just as nervous, and with as little luck. Not less.

We always had money for Grupp's, but not for the landlady or for grub. In a few weeks, Price and I moved to the parks.

Then Price got me a fight. He talked Billy Gibson into matching me with a 215-pound fellow named André Anderson. Nobody knew either of us. I went into serious training, knowing this was my big chance. I had to have food to build up my strength, more food than I could hope to buy.

I'd buy a nickel beer, if I absolutely had to. It was better, though, to wait things out in a busy bar and then grab a beer from in front of a talking drunk when the bartender wasn't looking. Then a slow walk, careless like, to the free-lunch counter. This was a crucial moment. If it was early in the day, the beer in my hand gave me the right to eat enough for my breakfast. The big problem was to eat breakfast nice and slow while stuffing enough for lunch into my pockets. I was glad I had fast hands.

After the roadwork in the parks, and the workout in Grupp's, I'd be starved again around suppertime. We tried different tricks. Sometimes Price would walk me in, whistle for attention and yell, "Folks, meet the next champion of the world." Everybody would look at me. I'd try to look tough. Now and then some fight fan at the bar would buy us a beer, and off I'd go for the free lunch while Price told the fellow all about me. I'd eat and eat and it got so I could guess within a mouthful when the bartender would holler, "All right, there, you now! Eat someplace else!" I'd stroll out, hoping they wouldn't notice that the "next champion of the world" had his pockets filled. Price would then take his shot.

I gained pounds on those free lunches and weighed 162 when I climbed into the ring to fight Anderson at Billy Gibson's Fairmont Club.

He knocked me down a couple of times in the first three rounds. Then I lost count. In the fifth he started to tire, probably exhausted from knocking me down. I gave him a real good pasting for the last five rounds.

There were no official decisions given in those days. Bets were paid off on the opinions of boxing writers. The bettors would mutually agree to pay off on how this or that writer saw the fight. These were called "newspaper decisions."

Damon Runyon was there that night, the first time I ever saw him. He thought I beat Anderson. So did most of the others. The *Morning World*'s expert was Ned Brown. He was to become my good friend and adviser. He thought I won too, and he wrote, "Dempsey is a great young fighter. There is one thing wrong with him, however. He looks like he needs a square meal."

Ned didn't know about the raids on the free lunches. But of course he was dead right. I needed a square non-pickled meal then and for some time after that.

Price and I got twenty bucks for that donnybrook. Two bucks went to the towel swinger in my corner. We split the remaining eighteen down the middle.

I did better than that in Cripple Creek.

Those park benches were making Price homesick for his bed back home. But he stayed a couple more weeks and put me in there against Wild Bert Kenny. I didn't know it, and Price didn't either, but I was picked to fight Kenny because I was considered a soft touch. Kenny was being built up into a box office attraction and he needed some more knockouts on his record.

Kenny and I earned our money that night at Gibson's. I dropped him in the second. He bounced me off the floor a couple of times in the third. By then we had learned each other's strong points and weaknesses, and for the next seven rounds I fought one of the most brutal fights of my life.

Every newspaperman at ringside gave me the decision. Gibson gave me thirty dollars. Two dollars for the towel man, and fourteen each for Price and me. I could have sold the blood for fourteen dollars.

Price had had all he could take of sleeping in parks and eating out of his pocket. We shook hands goodbye. He took a ferry to Jersey and a westbound freight.

It was lonely in the park that night without Price. I kept thinking that maybe I should have had sense enough to go home with him. But I had to stick it out and make the grade. At least, I said to myself, I can be my own manager now and keep all or most of what I make.

I was wrong, as usual. The next day when I went to Grupp's a guy I never liked much, named John the Barber, called me over to him and told me he was my new manager.

I told him what he was full of.

John the Barber— real name John Reisler— pulled a paper out of his pocket and told me to read it.

Jack Price had sold my contract to this guy for fifty bucks. I screamed that the piece of paper wasn't any good because Price had no contract on me to sell. Ours had been just a handshake deal. But nobody paid any attention. John the Barber had me.

He got his name from the big barbershop he owned on Broadway. He was a gambler principally, but he liked to strut around the fight game. I'll never know how he did it, but he became manager and business adviser to one of the greatest of them all, Sam Langford. Years later, Al Laney of the New York *Herald Tribune* found Langford blind and starving in a Boston cellar, which could give you some idea of how John the Barber managed his affairs.

My new manager was all business that first day he took

over. "Jack," he said, after I had cooled down a little, "we're going to make some real money. I've already got you a fight up in Boston."

Naturally, I was curious. And pleased. "Yeah? Who do I fight?"

John the Barber grinned. "Sam Langford," he said.

I just looked at the guy. "He'd kill me," I said.

He gave me a long song and dance about how good I was and what a win over Langford would mean. It made me sick to think he was talking about his own man, who had put thousands in his pockets.

"I've seen Langford," I said. "You're wasting your time. I won't fight him. He's too damned good for me."

John the Barber always had something else up his sleeve.

"All right, just as you say," he said. "How about Gunboat Smith?" He was still grinning.

Gunboat Smith could box rings around me and he could hit like a mule's kick. The papers had called him "the white heavyweight champion" before Jess Willard beat Jack Johnson the year before.

I shook my head again. Smith could lick me, I knew. But I wasn't afraid of him, as I was of Langford, I just didn't see any sense in a kid just out of his teens fighting a real pro who could disgrace him. I'd take Smith in time, and did, but this wasn't the time to try it. Langford I could never see myself beating.

Now I had turned down the first two fights John the Barber offered me. There's nothing braver than a manager sending his fighter into a ring to be killed. I was sick inside, standing there in front of him. Sick of failure, sick of being on the bum, homesick for my mother and for the days when I could make maybe fifty dollars among decent people. I wanted John the Barber to call me yellow. Just once. I wanted him to call me yellow because I wanted to hit him. And if I had hit him I never would have stopped until I had killed him.

Instead, he shrugged and walked away.

I couldn't force myself to go back to Grupp's for three days, but when I did, there was John the Barber, waiting for me with a big grin.

"Got a good fight for you, son," he said. "Up at the Harlem Sporting Club. We get twenty-five per cent of the gate."

"Who?"

"John Lester Johnson," he said, like he was telling me some happy news.

I looked at him a long time before I said, as quiet as I could, "You dirty no-good louse." Then I waited, but he was a conniving fight manager. He did nothing about the insult. He knew and I knew he had me in a terrible corner. All he had to do was tell the promoters around town, "This bum of mine is yellow; he won't fight nobody," and I'd have been blacklisted.

"Okay," I said. "I'll fight him. When?" I knew he could beat me. He could lick Gunboat Smith, and he had fought Langford a number of times and even beat him once or twice. He was one of the leading contenders for the heavyweight title. But I was in a corner.

John Lester Johnson gave me a worse beating than Sudenberg did. It was a lot more painful, too. In the second round he hit me the hardest punch I ever took, and that includes everybody who ever hit me anytime, anywhere, and with anything. It was a right to the body. It busted three ribs like matchsticks.

The easiest thing about being a prize fighter usually is the fighting itself. In the heat of a fight you forget that you may have thrown up in the dressing-room toilet before you went on, from nervousness and tension. You don't have time to think about how you're going to feel later if you lose— the humiliation, the disappointment, the frustration, and the why-didn't-I-do-this? second guessing. In a fight, a punch on the chin that knocks you down is painless. You laugh off the same punches that hurt you in the gym, during training for a fight. You don't laugh off a good punch in the stomach, that's true, but generally the excitement makes the pain secondary.

But the night John Lester Johnson caved my ribs in with one punch I was in agony. Every movement I made after that was just plain hell. In the late rounds of the first fight with Sudenberg I at least had the break of being out on my feet. I was unconscious, standing upright. When Firpo bounced me out of the ring on my head, at least I was dizzy enough not to care what happened after that. But I was clearheaded every awful second of the rest of the fight with John Lester Johnson.

When Bill Brennan had my ear hanging on shreds of skin I was scared. I was scared I'd lose my championship, scared I'd lose my ear. But now, fighting John Lester, I was afraid he'd kill me. I knew something had broken loose inside me and I kept thinking that if he hit me there again it might push whatever was loose right into my heart or something. My God, it was a terrible feeling.

The only thing I could do was run, which hurt, and duck, which hurt worse, until the fifth. Then something in me made me fight back. I must have fought back pretty good. A couple of the writers thought I deserved the decision. Two more called it a draw. The rest, eight or ten, were damn well right— they said I had been beaten. I wasn't beaten, I was massacred.

The crowd gave me a real good hand at the end. It was the first time I had looked at it. It was a full house. John the Barber had guessed $500, minimum, for our 25 per cent if the house was full. So the sight of it was some consolation.

John the Barber came into my dressing room while they were taping up my ribs.

"Nice fight, kid," he said, smiling all around his cigar. He went into his pocket, pulled out a roll and counted off thirty-five dollars.

I couldn't talk. I just looked at him.

"Our cut was only a hundred and seventy," he said cheerfully. "That's eighty-five each, less the fifty bucks I let your last manager have. The guy who went home."

"But he sold me to you," I said. I was so beat and helpless.

John the Barber shook his head. "Nope," he said, "he borrowed fifty against your next fight."

I put out my hand and took the money. I even said, "Thanks," from force of habit.

Well, I could get a room, but it wasn't much comfort. I

kept thinking, thirty-five bucks for three broken ribs, plus; ten bucks a rib, two-fifty for each black eye. The rest was for free. I couldn't figure which was worse— this or the manager in Goldfield who blew my dough shooting craps while I was unconscious. Then I decided that this was worse. The guy in Goldfield was at least human. John the Barber wasn't.

I dropped by to see him a couple days later.

"I can get you Langford," he said, as I walked in.

I didn't even get mad. "I can't fight anybody for a while," I said. "I'm going home until these things heal."

John the Barber was a sportsman. I had heard him say it many times to boxing writers, and some of them even printed it, like saps. I waited to hear him ask what he wasn't going to ask: "Need any dough to get home?"

"Well, kid," he said, turning back to the papers on his desk, "let me know when you're ready to fight again."

I walked out, crossed the Hudson, climbed on a pair of rods moving west, and went home to Salt Lake City. Try riding the rods from the Atlantic to Salt Lake with three broken ribs sometimes. Try getting them to heal while shoveling in a copper mine.

As soon as I felt the ribs were back in place, I took a fight. It was in Salida, Colorado, against a fellow named Young Hector. I had to get rid of him as quick as I could, for he might have hit me in the ribs again. They were back in place but they were still sensitive as boils. I belted him out in three.

I got $250 for that fight, and there was no manager around to protect my interests, as they always said. I gave my mother a hundred. Then I bought an upper back to New York and John the Barber.

He was glad to see me. "Got you a good fight, kid," he said. "Langford. Up in Boston. A thousand in it for us, easy."

The wind went out of me.

"He's too good for me now," I said.

John the Barber stopped smiling for a change.

"Listen," he said, "you fight who I tell you or you don't fight. I tell you now you're fighting Langford."

I guess that was the time to kill him. But something stopped me. Instead, I called him every foul name I had picked up in the mines, the jungles and on the rails of the West. He listened to me until I ran out of breath.

"You fight Langford or nobody," he said.

I headed back west in a "lower berth"— on the rods. It was December. That's not the best time to ride the rods, as I said earlier.

In Kansas City, looking for anything before going on west, I heard that Carl Morris wanted sparring partners. He was going to fight Frank Moran.

He gave me a job. Morris was a top fighter who weighed 235 and stood six feet four. I was paid seventy-five cents a day to let this big guy practice on me. I was up to 170 now. The rules were simple. If I dumped him on his can, I'd be fired.

I had a quarter in my pocket. I wasn't going to try to drop him. At least not then.

CHAPTER **6**

I DIDN'T SAVE ANYTHING ON THAT
salary of six bits a day. A quarter went for a flop. I blew
the other fifty cents on food. There was never enough.

On the night of the second day of my job I was in a
coffee-and-doughnut joint with a quarter in my pocket.
Morris came in. I guess my face must have lighted up. He

had earned thousands of dollars in his time, and this seemed to be just the right time to con him into buying me a dinner.

He sat down next to me and ordered coffee and dough-nuts, the same as I had. I knew the total check for both of us would come to twenty cents. So I tossed my last quarter on the counter, called to the counterman and said, like a big sport, "It's on me, Carl."

The Sepulpa Giant, as the papers called him, had a prissy kind of way. He said, "Oh, no. I never allow any-body to pay my check. You pay yours and I'll pay mine." I was looking to beat him out of a steak or something, and I couldn't even beat him out of coffee and doughnuts.

Boxing with him the next day in the gym I discovered something that almost took my breath away. I could beat him if I wanted to. I could beat Carl Morris, one of the top heavyweights in the world! I saw openings so clearly that it took all the strength I had not to do something about them. I needed that seventy-five cents a day, plus the extra dime he was now paying me for rubbing him down after he had worked me over. There was an acre of him to rub for that dime.

The whole match blew up on my fifth day on the job. Frank Moran hurt his hand and the fight was called off. I was out of work.

It was New Year's Eve when I got the news, and I had the crazy idea that I could substitute for Moran. I went looking for the promoter, and that wasn't easy. We didn't exactly travel in the same set. By the time I located him, he was at a New Year's Eve party in a fancy hotel. I didn't even have a shirt, just an old white sweater. I kept my ears warm by pulling my cap down over them. I don't remember what kind of pants and shoes I had when I went to the hotel to find him, but you can imagine.

Nobody stopped me as I walked across the lobby of the fancy place. Nobody stopped me until I got to the dining room where the party was being held. There was a hatcheck girl there. She stared at me, and no wonder. In addition to the getup, I had a busted nose and a tight haircut and, as usual, I needed a shave.

"Check your cap?" she asked. She probably thought it was a masquerade party. I handed the cap to her and she gave me a check— the first I had ever had.

I walked straight to the promoter's table. It took a lot of guts. Everybody was dressed, the women in evening gowns and the men in dinner jackets. I was red as a beet with embarrassment, but he was a gentleman.

"Hello, Jack," he said. "What can I do for you?"

I blurted the words. "Please put me in there in Moran's place," I asked him. I was pleading. "I swear I'll give you a hell of a— I'm sorry— I mean a wonderful fight. I think I can flatten this son of a— I'm sorry— I think I can lick Morris. Please . . ."

He patted me on the arm, shook his head and said, "Jack, I'm sorry. But I can't. I admire your spunk. Morris weighs two-thirty, and you just don't have the reputation to justify my prices or to be given a main event against a fellow like Morris. I'm really sorry."

He was, too.

People all around the room were looking at me now. I never felt so small, so helpless, so poor, so hungry. I could have eaten all the food at that table. I turned and walked out.

The hat-check girl was waiting for me, with my cap. I had a dime and a penny in my pocket. I took the cap. I was all confused, and sick inside. I put what I thought was the dime in her hand and started across the lobby. She let me go about twenty steps before she called me.

"Hey, you bum," she said. It could only mean me, so I turned. She beckoned for me to come back and I did. She handed me back the coin I had given her.

"Take this penny and buy yourself a cheese sandwich," she said. "You look like you need it."

I walked over to the closed gym that night and left a note for Morris. It said, "Please send my gloves, shoes and pants to me care of Martin's Saloon, Pueblo, Colorado."

I climbed on the rods and headed west. There was no particular reason for picking Pueblo except that I had been there before and might find some work there, and it was far from Kansas City and farther from New York. It was the coldest, most miserable ride of my life. John the Barber had put me on those rods, and I cursed that guy as I hung on to the cold steel.

When I got to Pueblo I looked up a friend named Liz Fisher (male) and he became my manager. Anybody could become my manager and most guys I met did, sooner or later.

Neither of us got rich. In fact, I started out in Pueblo as clean as I'd ever been, and nobody could get broker than I was. I went around to the saloon to pick up the package of gear Morris had expressed to me— and guess what? The big clown had sent it C.O.D. The charge was eighty-nine cents, and the cheap, stinking chiseler hadn't paid it— though I had let him belt me around for days for seventy-five cents and had rubbed him for a dime.

I stood there in the bar with my neck getting redder and redder. I didn't have eighty-nine cents. I didn't have a penny. I had to go around the town, bumming dimes and quarters when I couldn't find work, to raise enough to pay the parcel post on my stuff.

Someday . . . someday . . . I kept saying to myself, and the word ate up my insides. The "someday" began to mean Morris.

When I got my shoes, trunks and worn-out ring shoes back, I said to Liz, "Let's get out of here. Come to Salt Lake with me and see if we can get lucky."

Fisher had a reasonable question: "What'll we get there on?"

"The rods," I said. Then I realized he was one of my few friends who had never gone that way. I promised him I'd show him how, and I almost got him killed.

It was bitter cold the night we left Pueblo. The damned thing never wanted to stop. It was all I could do to hold on myself; for Liz it had to be the worst night of his life. I could hear his teeth chattering even above the clatter of the wheels and the creaking of the old cars swaying above us. I don't know how he made it. But he did, for at daybreak the brakes went on and we rolled out from under to find ourselves on the edge of some little town in Colorado. Liz was still shaking with the cold and the fright. I found us a jungle and put him up next to the bindle stiffs' fire, and then I went off into town to look for something to put in our bellies. We weren't hungry; we were starving.

I walked up to the best-looking house in town and knocked on the door. It was opened by as beautiful a young woman as I ever saw before or after that. I made my little speech about chores. She said she had none, but asked me to wait. She closed the door and was gone long enough to make me think she might be calling the cops. I was just about to run when she came to the door again and handed me a big paper bag.

It was a banquet, not a handout— ham, turkey, cheese, rolls, bread, fruit. I mumbled my thanks, tipped my cap and started trotting back to the jungle.

Tough as things got at that time in my life, I never got over being a practical joker. But a stunt I pulled that morning almost made me give it up. I hid the bag of food just before I walked into the place. Liz was still shaking. He looked up at me from his place near the fire. The poor guy was like a hungry animal.

I shrugged, meaning "No luck." Then I said, "We'll just have to get moving again."

It was one of the few times in my life I ever saw a grown man cry.

I was too stupid, too accustomed to this kind of life and

this kind of setback, to understand the kind of effect it would have on a man who was sensitive enough not to know how to exist like a bum.

I got that food bag pronto and spread it before him, while I tried to apologize. I didn't know how to.

Liz wouldn't touch the food until he had said a prayer of thanks. He waited for me to join him praying, and I did. Then we ate it like a couple of lions.

It made us feel so good that we decided to go on that night, cold or no cold. Instead, we wound up in jail.

The local police hit the jungle from all four sides and lined us up. There were half a dozen or so of us. The cop in charge went down the line, saying, "We want you . . . and you . . . and you there with the beard." I was the one with the beard. Liz got chosen too. They wouldn't tell us why we were being pinched. They just marched us off to the lockup.

A fellow on the bum gets tossed in the can a lot, and after a while nothing much surprises him. But the reason for our arrest this time surprised even an old hand like myself. The town had run out of pin boys. The local big shots had a bowling tournament scheduled and they had sent the cops out to round up a few bums to set pins— for nothing.

I was a pretty good bowler, and I had set pins before. But the bindle stiff working the next alley should have been a plumber. He dropped one of those big balls on my hand trying to put it back in the return groove. It mashed two fingers on my right, and they began swelling up around the fingernails. Terrible pain, really.

I walked up the alley and showed the hand to the cop in charge. He freed me.

I needed a doctor, but doctors cost money. So while Liz finished out the evening's free labor I sat off in a corner with a borrowed penknife. I bored holes in my nails to let the blood out.

Then I headed home to Salt Lake City, dirty, broke, unshaven and with a bum mitt— the end of a trip to New York. I had been young enough and crazy enough to think the trip would make my fortune. But I was closer to being a bum when it was over than when it started.

And there was Maxine to face.

Maxine was the first of what turned out to be three strikeouts at marriage. We were married in 1916 after my first trip to New York, when John Lester Johnson bashed in my ribs.

Maxine Cates came from Walla Walla. She played piano in a Commercial Street, Salt Lake City, saloon. In court in 1920 it was stated she had another profession. I married her as a piano player.

In 1920 Maxine took an oath in the U.S. District Court at San Francisco to the effect that she had continued her profession in 1916 and for several years later, which meant, or was intended to mean, that I falsified my draft papers, in which I swore— truthfully— that I was her principal support, just as I was of my mother, father, brothers, sisters and so forth.

To this day, I swear I don't know what pressures she was under when she testified. What I do know is that her testimony did me terrible damage which haunted me through most of the rest of my boxing life. She must have known it would, so all I can say today is that she must have been under a lot of pressure, like threats of prosecution if she didn't co-operate.

The reason I'm sure of this is that Maxine was a fine woman.

I was almost fifteen years younger than Maxine. She worked all the time. I traveled most of the time, trying to scrape a buck. I didn't see her for months on end. If I could have afforded to take her out of the saloon, things might have been different. It would have been tough at that, for she loved the life, the excitement. By the time I could afford it and show her a little excitement myself, the marriage was hopelessly lost in separations, two completely different ways of living, and— on my part— jealousy. I was very jealous of Maxine.

She crucified me on a witness stand in later years, but I never hated her. I never hated her because once I loved her very much, as any man loves his wife. And she loved me.

We were divorced after a couple of years. And hardly a couple of months together, as man and wife.

Liz Fisher's people, nice people, fed the wrinkles out of my belly, but Liz had had enough of me and I couldn't blame him. My next manager turned out to be a fellow I had known a little in Pueblo, fellow named Fred Windsor, called Windy, which he was. I was still trying to heal my busted fingers when I got a wire from him, asking me if I wanted to fight Jim Flynn in Murray, Utah. Wire collect, one way or the other, he asked me.

Fireman Jim Flynn, as they called him, was rated right up there with Gunboat Smith, Carl Morris, Frank Moran and Bill Brennan. As I read and reread the telegram I got some of the feeling I had had in New York when John the Barber kept trying to push me in there against Langford. But the more I thought about Flynn the more I thought about Carl Morris, who was considered his equal. I didn't think I could lick Flynn but I knew damned well I could beat Morris, just because I was so burned up over that eighty-nine cents — or the principle of the eighty-nine cents. So I wired Windy "Okay."

About four hundred fans showed up the night of the fight to see one of the most famous fights of my life.

Flynn knocked me out in two minutes of the first round. It was the only official knockout of my prize-fighting career.

In the first minute of the fight he hit me with a right that put me on the deck. I came up groggy and he was waiting there over me, and down I went again when he hit me. I got up and this time I was able to hold. But only for a few seconds. He knew how to get out of a clutch like that. He broke away, stepped back, threw a punch, and I was flat on my back a third time. When I got up I couldn't see him. He was behind me. I turned like a drunk, I guess, and he let me have it while my eyes were trying to find him. I went down again.

As I got up to face Flynn, my brother Bernie, working in my corner, threw in the towel.

When the fogs went away I cussed him, my own brother. "Why? Why? Why?" I kept yelling at him, like he had double-crossed me.

Bernie had an answer. "Because he'd've killed you with another punch," he said.

I should've known better than to yell at him. Bernie was a pro. He was right. He didn't stop it because I was his brother; he stopped it because I was having my brains beaten out. If he worried about me being his brother he would have stopped the fight against Copelin in Cripple Creek, when I told him I couldn't go any further.

The whys and wherefores meant nothing. All that was important was that I'd gotten a chance I had been praying for and been knocked out in two minutes of the first heat. In five years of fighting I had licked a passel of ham-donnies, knocked out some ham-and-eggers— and met two first-class heavyweights, John Lester Johnson and Jim Flynn. Three broken ribs and a two-minute kayo.

A couple of nights later I heard a train whistle. A few days later I was in San Francisco looking for flop money. And then I found myself in the hold of a stinking little freighter, on my way to Seattle. I had to find a buck. I was now going to be a lumberjack.

CHAPTER **7**

LUMBERJACKING WAS TOUGH WORK. I liked it and had the rough-and-tumble life in the camps. But there was this feeling I had that one day, no matter what, I'd be the heavyweight champion of the world. I beat my way back south to San Francisco and found Windy Windsor.

He found me a few fights that didn't mean much. It didn't even matter much that I won them. I wasn't going anyplace. I kept moving, looking, fighting, working when I couldn't find a fight. I was working in a Seattle shipyard, catching hot rivets in a tin can, when I got a wire from my mother telling me that Bruce had been stabbed to death. She asked me to come to Salt Lake.

I couldn't raise enough for a ticket on the plush, so it was back on the rods for me. I couldn't find the right combination of trains and Bruce was buried before I got there. Three or four hours before I got there. I never felt lower.

I hung around Salt Lake City working at what I could get, trying to make a go of my marriage. It wasn't easy. Then, out of the blue, I got a letter from Jack Kearns. It was early 1917. He asked me if I was "interested" in fighting again— as if I had been retired from the ring for ten years or so. I wrote back and told him I'd fight anybody anywhere anytime.

It was a compliment to hear from Kearns. I had had the saddest bunch of managers a fighter ever had, poor guys who were as hard up as I was. Kearns, at least, had a bankroll and also a stable of fair-to-middling meal tickets. He claimed to have been Bat Nelson's manager, and maybe he was. What was sure was that he was an expert at sending and taking American fighters to Australia.

I got a letter back from Kearns and when I opened it I got one of the biggest surprises of my life up until then. The letter invited me to come out to Oakland. There was something else in the envelope— a train ticket and a five-dollar bill. Imagine a *manager* putting out money to a fighter, a fighter who hadn't made him a nickel. It was too good to be true.

He amazed me even more when I showed up at his home in Oakland. He had a fight for me— a rematch with Willie Meehan. Willie was a fat little clown with a wonderful sense of humor. He could box very well, but his popularity around the Bay Area was based on the fact that he could make any audience laugh.

I got $250 for the fight, which was called a draw. The money was a godsend, but still I was disappointed and embarrassed that I hadn't done better for Kearns. But Kearns wasn't the least bit upset. He put me in there with a couple of fellows you never heard of, and then apparently he decided that the time had come to find out. He matched me against Gunboat Smith in San Francisco, in a California Law four-rounder.

In the first round I did very well against a man I once had feared and now only respected. In the second round Gunboat hit me a shot on the chin that almost tore my head off.

The next thing I knew I was riding the Oakland ferry-boat. I looked around. I was sitting next to Kearns and my second, Spider Kelly. Kearns was talking, as usual. I interrupted him.

"Smith was just too tough for me, Jack," I said. "I hope this isn't the end of the road with us."

Kearns looked at me, surprised. "You were great, kid. Absolutely great."

I couldn't understand how he could take it so lightly.

"What did he hit me with in the second?" I asked, down in the dumps.

"A right, kid," Kearns said enthusiastically. "I swear to God I thought it'd kill you. But you damn near killed him."

"I what?"

"Kid," he said, slapping me on the back, "you're going to be champion of the world, and I'm the guy who's going to get the title for you. We're off to the races now. Beating Gunboat makes you, don't you realize that?"

"Who beat Gunboat?"

Kearns knew enough about fighters to recognize what was wrong with me. He said, quietly for him, "Jack, where are we?"

"On the ferry to Oakland?" I asked.

"Who's he?" He pointed to Kelly.

"Spider," I said. "What the hell are you driving at?"

He shook his head. "Jack," he said, "you won the fight tonight. You won it!"

I thought Gunboat had flattened me for good with that second-round punch.

This unconscious win made me something of a big-timer, and it got me three of the most satisfying fights I ever had. They were all against the same guy, the only fellow I ever fought that I wanted to murder.

I was standing in the lobby of the Continental Hotel in San Francisco one day, before the first of these three fights, when I got a slap on the back that almost knocked the wind out of me, I turned around and looked up. It was Carl Morris, grinning down at me.

"Hi'ya, Jack," the guy roared. "Who'd've thought I'd be

coming 'way out here to fight my old sparring partner."

I tried to keep my voice from going too high, but it did, as it always did when I was excited.

"Listen, you cheap chiseler," I said, "you knew I was broke when you sent me my stuff C.O.D. I let you almost kill me for six bits a day, and you wouldn't give me a lousy little break like a few stamps."

Morris wasn't bothered. "Why the hell should I pay my money for your stuff?" he asked me. "But now calm down. That was some time ago. I'm going to do you a favor out here, Jack. We'll just give them a good show, and I won't knock you out."

"Knock *me* out!" I yelled. The whole lobby was listening now. You could hear me a block, I guess. "Knock *me* out! Why, you big bum, I'm going to murder you. I'm going to knock your goddam block off."

In the ring, I tried too hard. I did a pretty good job on him and won the decision, but it wasn't good enough to suit me. I wanted more of him, and Kearns found the way.

In 1918 I was doing pretty good in the West when Kearns got a $750 offer for me to fight Morris in Buffalo for Charley Murray, a real fine promoter. I was in bed in a Buffalo hotel when Murray first saw me. I was skinny and had that busted nose. He sized me up for a good minute, and I put down the funny sheet I was reading. Then he turned to Kearns and said, "Jack, I'll pay your expenses back west for both of you if you'll call off the fight."

"Why?" Kearns and I asked together.

"Morris will kill this kid of yours," he said to Kearns. "He'll outweigh your boy forty pounds. I'm just getting going good here in Buffalo, Jack. A bad fight'll ruin me."

Kearns did all my talking in those days, but for a change I spoke up. "Mr. Murray," I said, "if anybody gets killed it'll be Morris. He don't outweigh me forty pounds, either. He outweighs me fifty, and I'll knock him right in your lap."

He shook his head. I couldn't convince him that I had given Morris a pretty good going over in San Francisco in four rounds.

"I know, I know," he said. "Morris was out of shape."

"You get out of shape with dames and whisky, Mr. Murray," I said, like an expert. "Dames and whisky cost money. That cheap bastard is always in shape."

Finally he shrugged and said, "Well, it's your funeral." Morris came into my dressing room before the fight.

"That thing on the Coast was a fluke, kid," he said. "A couple more rounds and you'd've been in trouble. Let's get ourselves a good payday with this one, without nobody getting busted up. We can get a return match."

I was always nervous before fights. This night I was sitting on the edge of my rubbing table, with my head down. When he finished his proposition I raised it, looked at him and said, "Get outta here, you cheap bastard, or I'll flatten you right now." He got out, shaking his head.

I'll say one thing for Morris. He could take a punch, and he took a lot of them that night. I had him glassy-eyed and wobbly near the end of each of the first five rounds, but he'd come out fresh after the minute's rest.

In the fifth I noticed that Murray had stopped flitting

around the ringside and was taking a seat close to the apron. Or thinking about taking one.

"Sit down, Mr. Murray," I yelled at him, "and I'll drop this slob in your lap like I promised."

I couldn't do it. In the sixth, Morris knew he was licked and took dead aim at me below the belt. It was a bull's-eye and he was disqualified right then and there. It was a familiar stunt in those days, called "fouling out," a dodge of fighters who knew they were beaten and would rather have a foul in their record than a loss or a knockout.

The rest of the country still couldn't believe I was beating Morris, and I'll admit a California Law four-rounder and a foul fight didn't sound very decisive. So a New Orleans promoter matched us, and I'll be damned if Morris didn't show up in my dressing room before the fight. But this time it was a different Morris.

"Jack," he said, sadly, "I'm all washed up. This is the end of the trail for old Carl. Take it easy tonight. Gimme a break."

I looked him over. He was in perfect shape. "Baloney, Carl," I said. "You're only a couple years older than me. You're in good shape. You'd kill me without blinking. You're going out tonight *before* you get a chance to sock me below the belt."

I took him out in less than a minute of the first.

He was the only fighter I ever felt that way about.

Kearns and I moved on to Chicago, and I began to learn how he operated. I had never seen anything like it. We didn't get a fight for months, and our dough ran out, but

Kearns kept putting up a big front. He kept a long line of boxing writers and sports columnists coming in to see me and talk to me— though he did most of the talking. I was his tiger from the West. He announced he was willing to bet $10,000 I could beat *two* guys the same evening.

When the writers would leave, I'd say, "Where the hell you gonna dig up ten grand, Jack? We ain't got ten cents."

He'd brush it off. "Nobody's got ten grand to bet, Jack. It's just publicity."

Some of the writers went for his con. Some called it exactly what it was. But they all kept writing about the Man Eater from the Golden West. They said I came from Seattle, San Francisco, Salt Lake City, and Provo. All wrong, of course, but they spelled my name right. Kearns had a little different story to tell each one of them. Sometimes the stories stuck. I still hear, as God's truth, one of Kearns's pipe dreams. He told one group of Chicago writers that he had personally developed my left hand.

"He was right-hand crazy when I got him," Kearns said that day, out of the blue. "I put him in a gym and tied his right behind him. Made him fight with only his left."

We weren't making a quarter but I could see we were moving up. I was getting a rep, and I tried to keep it on the square.

"What's this bunk about tying my right behind me?" I said to him one day when he had repeated it to another writer and the writer had gone off to write the story. "You know damn well I've got a hell of a left and always did have."

"Sure, kid, sure," he said, clapping me on the back. "It's

the old build-up. You do the fighting, I'll do the managing. They're printing this stuff all over the country. It's what we need."

He was so much smarter than I was. So one day, when he explained something to me that didn't make much sense but sounded like it made sense, I said, "Okay, Jack, you're the doctor." I was to say that many times, so many times that I shortened "doctor" to "Doc." And that name stuck to him and people came to call him Doc more than Jack.

Eventually we had to fight. We had to fight for two reasons. We had to eat and pay the hotel rent, and people were wondering whether I was just a bum with a good build-up. Kearns put me in there against Homer Smith, in Racine, Wisconsin. We were rated about equal at the time. Smith was a good fighter, and a fine hitter. But his biggest rep, in the newspapers, was that he was a model, clean-living young American. There had been pieces written about him never taking a drink in his life and never smoking a cigarette.

I'm afraid I struck a terrible blow against clean living. I flattened Homer in 1:55 of the first round.

We all came back to Chicago in the same Pullman drawing room. Kearns was busy spending our money, tipping big and ordering whisky and cigars. Homer took his defeat like you'd expect any clean-living American sportsman. Then he surprised us. He poured himself a big slug of whisky and lighted up a cigar.

At first I was sad and then I was disgusted at the sight of him. This big bum is just a faker, I said to myself. He's been parading as a clean-liver but he's nothing but a drunken bum. I should have flattened him with one punch.

We all went over to the Morrison Hotel when we got to town. We ordered coffee. We wanted some and the clean-living boy needed some. Lots, in fact. I watched him down one cup, two cups, three cups of the strong black stuff, and then a strange thing happened. He pushed back his chair, jumped up, took a fighting stance and roared, "Where's Dempsey? Lemme at him! I'll stiffen him!"

Poor Homer had just come to. He had been out of his mind for hours, ever since I had knocked him cold in Racine. The whisky and cigars he destroyed on the train were— I found out later— actually the first contact he had ever had with such stuff. He just didn't know where he was or what he was doing. It must have been a strange feeling to wake up with a hangover and never know where and how he got it.

We were rolling now. Ten days after this came the second fight with Morris— the foul one— and three weeks after that one Kearns put me into Milwaukee against Bill Brennan.

Bill was as nice a guy as I've ever met in my life. When he was a top fellow and I was a bum, during that first trip I made to New York, he gave me work as a sparring partner. He helped me eat and get a flop. He was a good-hearted, generous fellow, nothing like Morris.

But, like Morris, he came to my dressing room in Milwaukee just before the fight. I jumped down off the table and shook hands with him. He was a kind of hero to me. Either he or Fred Fulton, the newspapers said, would soon fight Jess Willard for the heavyweight championship.

Brennan gave me a big hug, like fighters do, and then his face went serious.

"Dammit, Jack," he said, looking at me and pointing at Kearns. "That butcher you've got as a manager shouldn't have signed for this fight. I didn't want it, but that lousy publicity he put out about you forced me to take it." He stopped a bit and then went on, like a father. "Jack, I'm gonna have to flatten you. I don't want to. You're coming along just great, and I'm sorry I've got to spoil it. But that big clown Fulton is ducking me. If I don't take you out big, Jack, Fulton will get that shot at Willard. So you gotta go. I hope you understand."

Brennan really wasn't trying to scare me. He was just sorry for a kid he liked.

I was always fidgety and mean as a bear before a fight. For a moment I had been just the opposite, for I was happy to see Bill— a good man and my friend. But now I was back in character.

"Bill," I said, "I'm no hungry bum no more. Don't worry about me. I'll knock you kicking in the first round."

Brennan burst out laughing. "Good, Jack," he said, hitting me on the back for encouragement. "Good for you. So long, and the best of luck tonight."

"Good luck to you too," I said to his back as he left.

I did knock him kicking in the first round. Bill got up glassy-eyed and wobbled through the bell. In the second I bounced him four times. Being Bill Brennan, he got up four times.

He stayed up until the sixth and took an awful lacing. In the sixth I unloaded a right for his jaw with everything

I had. It spun him completely around. He went down with his legs twisted. All over the hall you could hear his ankle break. The referee stopped the fight at once, thank God, because Bill was trying to get up. I don't know what would have happened if he had gotten to his feet.

It was all I could do to go to his dressing room, where they carried him after the fight.

Why?

Well, after I got the people off my neck in the ring and finished posing for the flashlights, I started down the aisle to go to Bill's dressing room. And then from both sides of the aisle I heard a word that was the worst word I was ever to know for years after that. I had grown up in a world where there were no new dirty words, or any too bad to use. But this was the worst.

"Slacker!" a guy in the middle of a row yelled at me. When I turned that way somebody on the other side of the aisle said, "Slacker, you were lucky to win."

I had been called everything. Believe me, everything. But not this. I wanted to eat them, but the man I admired most in fighting, Brennan, was in his room with a foot hanging loose from a broken ankle. There wasn't any blood in my face when I got there to see him, I was so wild.

He talked about the fight, nice and easy. It was a spectacular and important win for me, but it was Bill, with his broken ankle, who was most at ease. He had so much class! We talked for a time— I don't know what I said— and then I started out. As I got to the door he stopped me.

"Next time you get dumped, Jack," he said with a smile. I pushed through the crowd to my own dressing room and slammed the door. Kearns was there, telling some box-ing writers what he had in mind for me. This time I couldn't wait for them to leave.

"Did you hear it?" I said to him. I guess my voice got high again.

Kearns always had a long answer, full of double talk and assurances. This night he was a little unsure of himself.

"Yeah," he said.

"Anybody say it before the fight?" I was excited and paying no attention.

"Yeah, a couple," he said.

"You sent those papers in, didn't you?" I asked.

"Sure, kid, sure," Kearns said, patting me on the back.

"Well, find out what the hell's going on," I said to him. "I'm not a slacker."

And I wasn't. The story is long, involved, takes a lot of telling and I'm going to tell it. But I think it should be told in proper order, one thing at a time. That night of Febru-ary 26, 1918, should have been the happiest night in the life of a fellow who had ridden the rods, eaten in jungles, picked the fruit, tossed the beets, crawled in the mines, known what it meant to be hungry, been thrown in jail. Now I could take care of my mother, father, brothers and sisters and my wife. But I never felt worse, and nothing that Kearns or the others could say to me about beating Brennan made me feel any better.

I wanted to die, and for some years after that I wished I had died.

I still had the problem of making a living for myself, my family and, come to think of it, Kearns. The way to do it best and quickest, as always, was around New York.

But in New York there was John the Barber. Now that I was belting out some good ones, the Barber was interested in me again. He kept giving out stories that I belonged to him.

"Dempsey says he'll starve a year before he'll fight for you," Kearns told John the Barber. I would've, too. John the Barber sued us. The case came up in Milwaukee. The court found there was no contract. We won the case.

With that much out of the way, Kearns began lining up a lot of fellows for me whose names I've forgotten— all second-raters. I don't know where he found them, but they all went out in a round or two. There weren't as many of them as the record book says.

Then came the first of my two fights against Billy Miske. Billy was a fine fighter; big, tall, good-looking fellow who wore his hair in a pompadour. He was a Lith or a Pole and one of the best men I ever met. I trained hard for this one, and so did he. We stank out the joint. It was just one of those things. Our styles didn't make for a good match. Some of the papers called it a draw; some gave it to me. There were only two good punches in the fight. He landed the first one and I landed the second. He staggered a bit, I staggered a bit. But beyond that it was a real dull one.

But, as it turned out, the fact that it was a bore was a blessing in disguise. Fred Fulton, by now the No. 1 challenger for Willard's title, had shown no interest in fighting me until he saw what happened in the Miske fight. That reassured him that I was safe to fight.

It was a big one for me, in a lot of ways.

I went in training at Long Branch, New Jersey, under one of the best ever— Jimmy DeForrest. Kearns lined up good sparring partners for me, as usual, somebody as big and fast as Fulton was. I did roadwork on the beach, and in two months I was brown and tough and mean, I guess. I was never a good gym fighter, but before the Fulton fight I knocked out a big sparring partner named Battling Jim Johnson.

Jack Curley was the promoter. My guarantee was for $12,500, out of which Kearns would take half and "expenses." I knew exactly what I was going to do with my bit. My mother had her eye on a $5,000 home in Salt Lake City. And I was going to see she got it— the first home of her own.

I guess you can understand by now what that meant to her, and to me. It was the biggest thing in my mother's life. She did something, as a result, that was reckless for her. She went out and borrowed a hundred dollars for a down payment on the house. I couldn't help her. I was broke and so was Kearns. But the fight purse would take take care of everything.

On July 21, 1918, a week before the fight— which was to be held in Harrison, New Jersey— Kearns came to me and said, "The fight's off."

"Off! It can't be."

"These people can't get the guarantee up," he said.

"Take a percentage then, Doc. I've got to have this fight. How much of a percentage can you get?"

"Twenty-five per cent."

"What would that come to?"

"I dunno. Ten thousand, maybe fifteen, twenty."

"No matter what you get, Doc, take the fight. My mother's put a hundred bucks down on a house."

The fight went back on.

Then, three days before the fight, I sprained an ankle. But it got okay. I'd have fought whether it was okay or not.

Fulton was a pretty good fighter, rangy, nice left, and he could hit hard with his right if he got set. There wasn't any doubt that he was the No. 1 challenger. He had fought them all, and he had beaten Langford.

I waited for him to show me that big long chin, and he did after I reached a couple of times for his stomach. He stuck his left hand out to jab me. I crossed my right over his left and down he went. Just out cold.

It took eighteen seconds, including the ten to count him out.

The crowd went crazy, particularly the people who showed up more than eighteen seconds late.

My share came to a little over $5,000. I had fought four years without making that much. I took the first train to Salt Lake and bought that house in Murray, then a suburb but now a part of the city.

It busted me, but what the hell. It was the proudest day of my life, and of my mother's too, I guess.

CHAPTER 8

IT TOOK ME A YEAR AFTER I BECAME
the No. 1 challenger to get Willard into the ring.

In the meantime I had to eat, and so did the people
dependent on me.

Through the rest of that year of 1918, after the Fulton
win, I fought men like Terry Keller, Jack Moran, Porky

Flynn, Gunboat Smith for the second time, Billy Miske for the second time, and Carl Morris for the third. The best man I met during that stretch was Battling Levinsky, who went on to win the light-heavyweight title. He had never been off his feet. I knocked him out in three, in Philadelphia.

I lost one, too. Willie Meehan— fat little, funny little Willie— slapped me around for four rounds, as usual, in San Francisco. Everybody laughed, but mostly at me. The fight raised $18,000 for a Navy relief fund, and for that I was glad, though broke. What bothered me was how bad Willie had made me look. I took it out the next night on Jack Moran. Belted him out in one.

Is it possible to fight as much as I did at that time and still have the shorts? Yes. My goodness, yes. I wasn't champ, the gates were small or for charity, and Kearns liked to live as if we had it.

I remember that early in 1919 we were staying at the Claridge in New York and the manager was beginning to glare at us and make vulgar noises about money. One day Kearns said, "Want to make a quick hundred bucks?"

"What do I have to do?"

"Just take a bow. Can you bow?"

"Of course I can bow!" I said, steaming. "Look." I bowed.

Kearns looked at me like I was a worm, or something. "Why, you bum, you can't even bow. What kinda upbringing didja have? Not stiff. Graceful, like this." He taught me to bow.

Seems he had finagled a booking downtown in a burlesque theater. Personal appearance. We went down by streetcar, but three blocks short of the place he got up and said, "Come on, we get off here."

"Why here, Doc?" I asked. But he was busy calling a taxi. He pushed me into it, climbed in behind me and gave the guy the address.

"Never let 'em know you're broke, kid," he said. "Just never let 'em know a thing like that." Doc was speaking with as much experience, I guess, as any man could have had.

As soon as we stepped out of the cab, Kearns made a beeline for the manager. He wanted to collect the money in advance. I stood outside the place, enjoying a nice sign which read:

PERSONAL APPEARANCE

OF

JACK DEMPSEY
Next Heavyweight Champion of the World

Nobody gathered around me. I was just another guy reading a sign in a run-down section of town, though I guess I was the only fellow there with a dirty white sweater and a busted nose. Then I went inside and asked where the dressing room was. I found it, and it was full of girls. They were real nice to me. They thought I was a character.

Kearns bustled in. "They won't pay until after the show," he said, and I believed him. "Now, come on, we're going on stage."

He stepped out on the stage and got a tremendous hand.

I watched him from the wings, wondering how— and what— I'd do. Some of the people in the audience thought he was Dempsey. Doc made a terribly long speech. He was a real hambone. In winding up his talk he said, "This young man who will soon knock Jess Willard unconscious was born right here in the heart of New York City. He has Italian and Irish blood, but he is mostly Jewish."

It was the right part of town to introduce me as a Jew. I walked out in the blinding stage lights, bowed, and got a five-minute ovation. When it finished I just stood there. The place quieted down until it was like a graveyard. Then somebody yelled, "Speech! Say something!"

I was petrified. I couldn't open my mouth. I tried another bow. Somebody started laughing and it spread like a fire. The bums in the gallery began giving me the bird.

I certainly couldn't bow again. I was too terrified to try to say a single word, not even "Thanks." I could hear Kearns hissing from the wings, "Get off! Get off!" I couldn't move my legs.

They were beginning to throw things from the audience. I felt like I had been fouled. And I was. I had been hooked through the crotch by the long-handled hook used to get lousy performers off the stage on Amateur Night. The guy with the hook had tried to get it around my waist but missed. But it moved me. When I hit the wings I was running. The house roared with jeers and laughs.

I ran right out the stage door and hid in the first bar I could find. I was burning at Kearns, for getting me into a spot like that, and at myself, for being such an uncouth baboon.

After a bit, two old guys came into the saloon and stood up to the bar. They had just come from the burlesque house but didn't notice me. After a while, one of them spoke.

"If that Jew can fight I can make a watch," he said.

I, the No. 1 challenger for the heavyweight championship of the world, slept in Central Park that night. I was too embarrassed to face Kearns, afraid to have to stand there and see his contempt.

He was the boss. Period.

There were some tune-up fights, coffee-and-cake fights, leading up to Willard, one-round knockouts over Jack Hickey, Kid Harris, Kid Henry, Eddie Smith and Tony Drake— people like that.

Then the big break, even though the word "slacker" was still rattling around. Rickard got Willard's name on a contract.

This is as good a time as any to debunk some of the legends that have been accepted for years as the truth about the fight. The worst, of course, is that I soaked my hands in plaster of Paris after they were bandaged and before I put on the gloves. You know, I never needed anything like that.

Kearns and I signed the contracts with Tex Rickard in Hoboken. Boxing was still having its legal troubles in New York. I got quite a jolt out of being in the same room with Rickard. He carried a gold-headed cane and dressed like a rich rancher. I wondered if he remembered me from Goldfield years before, when Sudenberg had sent me "home" in a wheelbarrow. (He couldn't have, I found out later; he wasn't there at the time.) He was a friendly man and I could see he took a liking to me. Actually it wasn't just a liking. He was worried that Willard would kill me.

The fight was set for July 4, 1919. I signed for $19,000, half of which would be Kearns's. Willard, of course, was to get much more, which was right.

Kearns found me a nice training camp, with indoor and outdoor rings, at the Overland Club, Toledo, and I got down to work. I wasn't an easy fellow to train. I overdid everything, because I wanted to be perfect at what I was trying to do. I worked so hard that there was always a chance I'd get too fine, go stale. This time I knew I had to be righter than anytime before in my life.

As usual, Kearns lined up good sparring partners. I had Bill Tate, who was almost as big as Willard, and Jamaica Kid and a few others for speed. For my morale, I had old Battling Nelson. Bat lived in a tent at the scene of the fight, but he spent most of his time around my camp. He still wanted to fight, old as he was. After I'd finish working on the bags, he'd start pounding away at them, work up a sweat, take off his coat and shirt, and pound some more. He gave me a lot of confidence, Bat did. He kept telling me I'd lick Willard.

I couldn't wait to get at Willard, and one day I nearly did.

I had put a payment down on a Stutz Bearcat before going into training, and I had it with me at Toledo. I thought I was a smart kid and pretty good. One day before the fight I was driving along a road outside town and

I saw a big Cadillac ahead of me. I gave it the horn but the guy who was driving it wouldn't move over and let me pass, just stayed in the middle of the road. So finally I drew up beside him, damn near going into the ditch.

It was Willard. It burned the hell out of me. I said to myself, It's him or me right now. If he don't get over, I'm going to make him.

I did, too, without even scraping his car. Maybe that did something for me.

Still, not too many people thought I had a chance. The stories about the fight kept pointing out the difference in us. Willard stood half a foot taller and would outweigh me seventy pounds. In fact, there was so much written and said about it that Rickard had to weigh me in at a public ceremony.

I stuffed myself with bananas and put some rocks in my trunks and weighed 188 when I stepped on the scales. That seemed to reassure everybody.

Actually, I weighed 180— not even the 182 or 184 that the record books have sworn for forty years.

It was the hottest July 4 I could remember. Some said it was 100 in the shade; others said 110. All I know is that the resin boiled out of the bleacher seats and before the fight began they were selling hot "ice water" for a dollar a glass. They had run out of lemonade, but it wasn't much good anyway. Bat Nelson had gotten up early that morning and decided to take a bath in honor of the occasion. He looked around the grounds and found a nice big hogshead filled with what he thought was water. He scrounged some soap and took a nice bath in it. It was the lemonade.

I couldn't sleep, waiting for daylight to come. And when it came I couldn't wait to get to the arena. It was the longest morning of my life. But then it was time to go; time to get ready.

I went to my hot little dressing room, with Kearns and the guys around me, stripped down, got into my cup, my trunks, my socks and shoes.

Then, so the stories have said for years, I plastered my mitts until they became like two lumps of marble.

As God is my judge, it never happened.

It couldn't happen. First, I didn't need plaster and it had never occurred to me that I might, and, second, I couldn't have gotten away with it even if I had tried. Willard had a man in my dressing room, and Kearns had somebody in Willard's, checking. Willard's fellow was big Walter Monaghan. He stood over me as they taped my hands— so much gauze, so much adhesive tape. We each got the same. Monaghan stuck with me, right down the aisle and into my corner.

Willard kept me waiting. That can be torture when you're keyed up, as I was. And then he came into the ring like a moving mountain, dropped his robe, turned his back on me and held up his arms to the cheering crowd.

I thought I was going to get sick to my stomach. Kearns had kept telling me what a bum Willard was— big, fat, no good. Now as I looked up the wall of his back I could see he was in terrific shape. The way he was holding up his arms made his fists seem twice as high in the air as I was tall. The muscle stood out on his back. I looked at all six feet six and 250 pounds of him and I said to myself, This guy's liable to kill me.

During the instructions I kept looking at his belly. I hardly knew what the referee, Ollie Picard, said to us.

Then the bell. I almost ran at him. I stuck a few long ones at his body, weaving and bobbing. He reached down with a left jab and dropped his right to get set to throw a punch with it.

As he did, I straightened up instantly and hit him with a left hook on his cheekbone and temple. It busted his eye open and down he went, shaking the ring like an earthquake.

There was awful hollering and screaming and confusion. I felt like I wanted to get down there on the deck on top of him and beat him some more. One punch wasn't enough. But then he started to get up. I stood right over him and beat him to the canvas again. And again. And again. And again. And again. And again. These were the rules in those days.

I couldn't miss. Wherever I hit him, he lumped up or bled. It was a slaughter. When he went down the fourth time, Picard counted him out and raised my hand.

The whole place had gone crazy. You couldn't have heard a cannon go off. Kearns grabbed me, put his face next to mine and yelled, "Go on! Get outta here! Get to the dressing room!"

I stumbled down the ring steps and started up the aisle. A lot of guys were crawling on my back.

Then I heard Kearns screaming hysterically to me. I

turned around and he was waving to me to come back. I climbed back through the ropes.

"It's still on!" he yelled. Willard was sitting on his stool and his people were working on him.

"Okay," I said. For some crazy reason, I thought Kearns had brought me back to box a little more for the moving pictures— to make it look good.

"The bell saved him," Kearns said. "Nobody heard it. The round ended at the count of eight."

Suddenly I felt terribly tired, and punched out. The bell sounded and I came out cautiously. He hit me a pretty good right-hand uppercut that shook me up. This wasn't for the moving pictures. This was real, and I still had to win something I thought I had already won.

I boxed him through the second, but in the third I really gave it to him good. I don't know how he made it back to his corner. But he didn't make it out. They threw in the towel before the fourth could start.

That night I went to bed at ten o'clock, completely pooped. About midnight I had a nightmare. I dreamed that Willard had knocked me out. It was so realistic I fell out of bed.

I got up and turned on the lights and looked at myself in a mirror. I had dreamed I was all cut up around the eyes. There wasn't a mark on me.

I dressed in a hurry and went down to the street in front of the hotel. A kid was selling extra papers.

"Who won the fight?" I asked him.

He looked at me. "Aren't you Jack Dempsey?" he squeaked.

"Yeah."

"You damn fool, you did!" the kid said.

I gave him a buck, went back upstairs and to bed.

I was the heavyweight champion of the world. I thought of the hard days as a kid, the lonely nights in the jungles and on the rods, the barroom fights for food. Now it wasn't a case of saying, "I can lick anybody in the room." I could lick anybody in the world, and I had just turned twenty-four— and had all those good years left.

But one thing remained the same. I was broke.

A couple days before the fight, Kearns came to me. "You think you can knock this guy out?"

I said I thought I had a chance.

"You think you can knock him out in the first round?" he asked me.

"How the hell do I know?" I said, burned. "Why do you ask a question like that?"

Kearns was mysterious. "I've got a chance to bet ten thousand against a hundred thousand that you win in the first," he said.

Well, he did. At least, it was taken off the $19,000 guarantee. The expenses and extras ate almost all the other nine.

CHAPTER 9

I WAS FREE AS A BIRD. MAXINE AND I
had been divorced before the Fulton fight, when it didn't
seem that I'd ever make a buck. Now I had the title and
my first chance to live it up and learn something about the
way people lived on the other side of the tracks.

The first change I noticed in myself after beating Willard

was that I could talk to nice people. I hadn't met many along the line, but those I had met frightened me. They were always using words I couldn't understand. It was embarrassing to say something to them and see their faces go blank. It was embarrassing also when sometimes I'd bust out laughing at something decent they'd say, or some polite gesture they made.

So I had learned to shut up except when I was with other fighters, trainers, rubbers, or old pals.

But, suddenly, people understood me. They started laughing at my jokes. I could understand every word they said to me. And why not? I could have understood a college professor if all he talked about was how wonderful I was!

Women changed, too. Every "Hello, Mr. Dempsey" suddenly sounded real kind. And interested.

I was still a bum with a knife and fork, and I dressed like a guy an honest cop would arrest at a carnival. I had been wearing suits for two years and had been wearing a necktie for at least four years; but I dressed as much like Kearns as I could, and he was patent-leather-shoe-and-diamond-stickpin-happy. Rickard, who now was sure that I, not Willard, was the greatest heavyweight of all time (Jack Johnson had been, in Tex's mind, before Willard) also gave me some hints on how to dress, eat, talk.

Offers of all kinds began flooding us, and I was as eager as Kearns was to start cleaning up. But first I wanted to see my mother in Salt Lake City. It was a wonderful homecoming. One of the first things she said as I hugged her was, "Didn't I tell you, Harry?" She was remembering the book about John L. Sullivan she had gotten from the traveling salesman when she was carrying me, and her prediction to me as a boy.

My mother had some bad news too. She was going to divorce Pop, after all they had been through. My father had added girl chasing to some of his other sins against the church. My mother could stand a lot, but that was too much.

She wasn't bitter. Just firm. And she chuckled sympathetically when she told me this story about him:

The day I fought Willard the Salt Lake City *Telegram* had a direct wire from the Toledo ringside. The sports editor got the news off the wire and roared a blow-by-blow account of the fight to a crowd of more than five thousand gathered on Main Street between Second and Third.

Just before the fight started, somebody spotted my old man in the crowd. The fellow in charge invited him up on the stand, introduced him, and the crowd yelled for a speech.

My father hawked to clear his throat, then bellowed, "Friends, Harry's a good boy. He won't disgrace us. He'll do right well. But that fellow Willard is just too big for Harry. It'll be a good fight until the fourth round. Then Willard will knock out Harry."

When Harry did a little better than had been predicted, the happy crowd yelled for another speech from my father.

He climbed back on the stand, looked around the crowd happily and said, in his high voice, "Didn't I *tell* you my Harry would do it?"

Hollywood was next.

The movies had "discovered" me, and Kearns wasn't a guy to let them off the hook for making a mistake like that. He got us $1,000 a week from Pathé, and for the next few years in and out of the movie town I never worked for less and often worked for more.

My feelings about Hollywood were mixed. Something told me I wasn't going to be much of a threat to Henry B. Walthall. In my own class, however, I didn't turn out too badly. At least I was as good an actor as Jess Willard, who was out there before me, and as good as some of those who followed me, like Babe Ruth, Benny Leonard, Georges Carpentier and Gene Tunney. Which, of course, isn't saying too much.

The thousand a week was all the lure I really needed, naturally. But there was another reason I wanted to go there. I had been nuts about the movies, as a fan, since I was a kid. I had done everything but jimmy a window open to get into them when I didn't have the money. And when I did have the fare I'd sit there by the hour, hypnotized.

I was a cowboy picture fan, mostly. Maybe now I could even get to meet some of those fellows in person, I figured as we headed west. Maybe even Tom Mix, or William S. Hart, or Will Rogers.

You could've knocked me over with a feather when I stepped off the train. *They* had come down to the station to meet *me*. A few days later Mix, my hero, even stripped down and posed for pictures, as if he was going to box me. A beautiful build, by the way. I sparred a little with

Rudolph Valentino, who wasn't bad for an amateur. He couldn't knock your hat off, though.

I got to know them all. I didn't realize it at the time, but we all had a lot in common. Some of them were no better educated than I was. Some not even as well. We were all very rich— or were going to be— and we were all very famous because of freaks of nature. I was born with a good punch. They were born with good profiles, pretty mouths, curves in the right places, things like that.

I stepped into a life that was enough to make my head swim. This was the Hollywood before taxes, censors, reformers, sound, and such. Imagine a guy not too long away from Commercial Street in Salt Lake, and south of the Slot in San Francisco, and Skid Row in Seattle, actually escorting a star to a formal opening. Or taking some Hollywood beauty to dinner. Or sitting in a soft chair in a drawing room having a relaxed conversation with a famous producer or director. Or dancing with a glamorous starlet.

I went to Hollywood parties that people are still talking about, for they don't happen any more and haven't happened for years. I enjoyed every one of them. If they were orgies— as they came to be called in the papers— I sure didn't know. Everybody drank though. I never was much of a drinker. I was an amateur in the league I traveled in. I tried a little of everything, but usually wound up with beer. I had the first champagne of my life about this time. It tasted to me like citrate of magnesia, and still does. They drank wine at the formal dinners I went to, and that I liked. Except that it would make me sleepy just when the rest of them were ready to pile into their Pierce Arrows and Dusenbergs and cars like that and go on the town.

There weren't too many places to go. The Montmartre Café was the favorite. I took several of the top girl stars there. Every time we walked in, a photographer was waiting to fire away at us. I couldn't figure out how they knew when we had chosen that place to go, until I learned about publicity men.

If I had married every star the papers said I was going to marry two things would have happened. It would have been a delightful experience, and I'd have been arrested. I did get stuck on a couple of them and have reason to believe a few felt something more toward me than wanting my autograph. Nothing serious, though.

The girls kidded me a lot because I was such a lousy dancer. I could move my feet and legs in a ring as fast as anybody and faster than most. I had all the balance anybody could need, and the sports writers kept talking about the rhythm of my punches. On the dance floor I was a cow on ice.

I met the men of Hollywood too. Wally Reid, the best-looking and most reckless of them, was my close friend—to my sorrow in the years to come. I got along with Charlie Chaplin, and Douglas Fairbanks was my pal. If you were Douglas Fairbanks' pal at that time in Hollywood it was like having a credit card today, except there was no bill at the end of the month. If Hollywood knew that Fairbanks liked to have you around, all the others wanted you at their parties. If you were in a real classy inner circle, the sign of it was that Doug would goose you at parties— such as when you were trying to make polite talk or were about to accept a glass of champagne from an imported British butler.

Fairbanks made a production of the goose. He could hide behind a drapery for an hour at one of his own parties waiting for the right moment to slip out and apply the goose. Sometimes people got sore at him, but I could understand. I think I introduced the hot foot to the East Coast of the United States, when I was training for Fulton. I could hide under a table without hardly breathing while I bent a match, fitted it into a guy's shoe where the sole joins the body of the shoe, and light it.

What I liked about Fairbanks was that he took care of a lot of old fighters who had drifted out that way. He had Bull Montana and Spike Robinson on his regular payroll and would use fighters in every one of his pictures. The studio where I made a serial named *Daredevil Jack* (which was so bad they don't even show it on the Late Late Show) was right across the street from the studio Fairbanks and Mary Pickford had formed. In the back of the place, Doug had fixed up a small baseball diamond, basketball court, high jump, broad jump, horseshoes, things like that. I worked out there quite a few times.

For all the partying at night, I stayed in pretty good shape. I worked as long as fourteen hours a day, lousy as it was. It wasn't easy. Aside from the embarrassment of trying to make love to a girl in front of a camera and a lot of people watching, it was tough trying to pull my punches when the script called for me to fight an actor. It was tougher not knocking them out than it was flattening many pros I had tangled with.

When it wasn't Hollywood, around that period, it was Broadway. A heavyweight champion doesn't have to be lonely much around Broadway.

A fellow could eat at LaHiff's and learn a little from somebody with more brains, until it was time to take the car over to the *Follies* or the *Scandals* and pick up the second girl from the left. After that, it was any number of places— one night Perona's on Forty-ninth, or George La Maze's Park Avenue, or Jerry Docker's, a speak that didn't even bother putting a strong-arm fellow on the door.

After that, it would be on to the night clubs— Club Richman, Barney Gallant's, the Silver Slipper, Texas Guinan's, and so many others that came and went and came back again with different names but the same owners. These were the places where I'd see Kearns.

Jack was enjoying being manager of the heavyweight champion of the world even more than I was enjoying being the champion. I didn't know it then but we were already drifting apart. We were always with different groups. His would close the joints. Mine would leave at, say, two-thirty in the morning.

Harlem was a place the Broadway crowd went in those days, and I gave it a lot of my trade. It had Connie's Inn, Small's and, pretty soon, the Cotton Club.

It's hard for the new generation to understand, but it was very easy to be arrested in those days. It must be remembered that it was against the Federal, state and city law to serve or even consume booze, or even be caught in the same joint with sellers and drinkers if the cops walked in. One evening I was sitting with Al Jolson and Buddy De Silva, minding our business, in a place near 135th and Lenox. The cops beat the door in. As the cops came through one door I went out the other. I had been getting a lot of mail from kids and I knew it would look terrible to them if I was pinched in a speakeasy.

I ran through the miserable joint— could've broken a leg— and found the last thing I'd expect to find, a bedroom. I went under the bed, thinking, rich or poor, the cops always find Dempsey. This was no exception. A big Irish cop grabbed me by the ankles and dragged me out from under.

It was very embarrassing.

The truth is that most of the places I went to during that period— and I didn't go alone, of course— were owned by characters. I had known bums, tramps, chiselers, and what have you, but never the organized-mob fellows until this time. They were just beginning to show an interest in the fight game. That interest spread a lot more later, and it could have ruined it.

In those days the hoods operated differently. They weren't out for a buck, necessarily. They'd buy, let's say, $10,000 worth of tickets to a big fight and hand them out among politicians and rich guys. That brought them close to promoters, managers and fighters, and people with pull— decent people, I mean. And it gave them an out whenever they'd be picked up as "vagrants." They could always say, "I'm a prize fight manager already." Enough people would say yes.

Rickard was a fellow who wasn't fooled by these fellows. He wasn't even impressed by them. He had seen tougher bums for thirty-five years. Some of them tougher than anything New York ever produced.

He called me into his office one day. He was chewing his cigar. I sat down across the desk from him and he told me something I knew, for a change.

"Jack," he said, "those gangster fellers are nice guys, most of them. You're going to have to meet them more and more in this business. Be nice to them, polite, but don't never have no business with them. When they own you they don't let go. And tell that noisy manager of yours the same thing."

Tex wasn't too fond of Kearns. They had known each other as far back as the Alaska gold rush days.

I had some nice friends too. Real nice. A guy named Billy Seeman, for instance. Billy had a penthouse on Waverly Place, down in the Village. It became part of my education. I'd sit there at his parties, a guy with a flat nose and a quarter-inch haircut, and let experience rub off on me.

Billy's parties got them all, the people who made New York what it was at the beginning of the 1920's. I got to know Morton Downey there, and he was even shyer than I was. And Jessie Reed, Marie Wallace, Lillian Lorraine, Ruby de Remer, Bessie Love, Vivienne Segal, Madge Evans and Dolores— who had only that name and was the most beautiful show girl in town.

Also Bugs Baer and Rube Goldberg, Mabel Normand, Ethel Shutta, Paul Whiteman, Barbara Bennett, Tammany Young, Joe Schenck, Mark Hellinger and Jimmy Walker. Lots of others, too— O. O. McIntyre, Strangler Lewis, Claudette Colbert, Colleen Moore, Jack White, Sylvia Sydney, Peggy Hopkins Joyce, Bert Lahr, Grantland Rice, Laddie Sanford, Billy de Beck, Fred and Adele Astaire and the Dolly Sisters, to name a few.

Billy's place always drew the best-looking women in New York, the funniest stage and night club clowns, the top newspapermen, politicians, society people. I just listened. It was like going to the most interesting school in the world, a school where all the professors drank, laughed, knew all the ropes.

I could have gone on like that indefinitely. But the papers were beginning to give me the bird for not defending my title.

On March 5, 1920, I made my first defense, but there wasn't any risk involved. I fought an old pal named Terry Keller in Los Angeles. We boxed three harmless rounds. It was more of an exhibition that a fight.

Terry was a character. I lost track of him after that fight until the late 1930s. I was booked to make a talk at a Kiwanis dinner in California. On the afternoon of that day I learned from an old fighter that Terry was in a mental institution in the same town. I dropped by to see him. A fellow in a white coat took me to the asylum's kitchen, and there was my old pal, working on the pots and pans.

I walked over to him and said, "Hello, Terry, how the hell are you?"

He stared at me for a moment and then said, heartbroken, "Jack. Oh, Jack. They got you, too." He put his arms around me. "When did they nab you, Jack? But that don't matter. Take off your coat, Jack, and I'll see that you get a good job here. With me."

I finally convinced Terry that they hadn't gotten me. Yet. And I was able to spring him for the evening, in my custody.

Terry sat next to me on the dais that night and I had him introduced as my friend, a great old fighter. He got a real kick out of it. Not a soul in the room knew. After the dinner we had a few drinks, talked fights for a couple of hours, and I took him back to the place. He died there not too long after that.

But that visit with Terry Keller was a good many years in the future. The big worry of my life, the thing that had been eating me out since I first heard the word "slacker," was coming to a head.

I was to stand trial in Federal Court, San Francisco.

The honeymoon was over.

CHAPTER 10

A "NO" THAT SHOULD HAVE BEEN A
"yes" and a "yes" that should have been a "no" almost
ruined me. I gave the wrong "no" in San Francisco in 1917
and the wrong "yes" in Philadelphia a year later. We were
at war with Germany throughout this time.

The "no" came first. In 1917, two years before I won

the title, a San Francisco sports editor who had consistently blasted me, asked me to fight for a charity sponsored by his paper. I refused. It would be easy now to say I turned him down because of a previous engagement. Or there was some mix-up. I must have been pretty steamed at him, for up-and-coming fighters don't often say no to a powerful sports editor.

He never forgave me, and in time he got his revenge. Damned near destroyed me.

Now for the fatal "yes." One day in Philadelphia a government man came to my hotel and asked me to co-operate with his bureau's efforts to encourage more men to go into war work. I said sure. He wanted a picture of me in a shipyard. I drove out to the Sun Shipyard, put a pair of overalls on over my regular clothes and posed for the stupidest picture any man ever posed for. But I didn't realize it at the time. The government man shook my hand and thanked me. He said it would help the war effort. Kearns, my brain, had no objection.

I forgot about it— until the next day. The papers used a full-length shot. It showed my patent-leather shoes sticking out of the bottom of a workingman's overalls.

A lot of writers gave me hell, and the public took up the cry.

It's tough to be an athlete in wartime, particularly if you're a well-known one and you have a legal reason for not being in uniform. The picture of shoe clerks with eyeglasses marching off to war, while some big pitcher keeps pitching or some rough-looking boxer keeps boxing, is hard to understand or stomach. It's particularly griping for mothers, wives and sweethearts of the men who get called.

In World War I and the bigger one that followed, lots of people forgot that the laws of the land provide no favors either for the shoe clerk or for the athlete. If a man is physically fit and has no legal right to postponement or deferment of enlistment, he goes. In one way, the athlete gets a little the worst of it when Selective Service steps in. Injuries or dependents claimed by the shoe clerk are believed quicker than if a star athlete claimed them.

Of course, we've got no monopoly on that. Les Darcy, a great Australian fighter, found that out. There was a law in Australia, clear and known to all, that any Australian who was out of the country before the start of World War I was not required to return home and join a service.

Les was in America when the Aussies went to war. He fought here. The newspapers back home crucified him. They hounded him until his death, in Memphis. It has always been said that Darcy died of a broken heart: I know the doctors say that's impossible, medically. But I wonder if they're sure. I'm not. I went through a lot of the same beating that killed Les.

Of course, Darcy's humiliation and my own could have been easily avoided by joining up. There are two main reasons why a man doesn't volunteer in time of war but waits his turn under Selective Service. He is either afraid of getting killed or he is afraid of losing his income.

Nobody wants to get killed. But I was in little danger of any wound except maybe a bloody nose if I had enlisted. It was a hundred thousand to one that I would have spent the duration doing just what I did in civilian life— fighting with gloves on. That's what almost all name boxers wound up doing in both wars, just as most big-league ballplayers spent their time playing ball. There were great exceptions like Ted Williams and Bob Feller, for example. But not too many.

As for the money, I was just getting enough of it to take care of my family and get the wrinkles out of my belly.

The Draft Act of World War I gave the draft boards the power to decide whether a man belonged in the service or at home. I followed the law. My draft board never called me. It never called me because it felt I was entitled to deferment.

I was never charged with failing to register for the draft, which is draft dodging in its basic meaning. I was charged with defrauding the government in connection with the papers I filled out. The public had a quicker way of saying it. I was charged with being a slacker.

God only knows how many people called me that— yelled it, loud and clear, in front of thousands of people in fight crowds or theaters. People would yell it from passing automobiles, or call it out a window as I passed.

But a funny thing: Nobody ever called me a slacker to my face. Those thousands of people who elected themselves my judges handed down their decisions from a safe distance. Nobody ever made the charge in print. But they hinted at it in a way that said as much but was libelproof.

I got so damned fed up that I decided to join the Navy. I talked it over with a pal of mine I had helped with refereeing jobs around the Great Lakes Naval Training Station, Commander Jack Kennedy. Kennedy was happy about it. Great Lakes had the best boxing team in the world— fellows like Harry Greb and Pal Moran— but it needed a heavyweight.

Kennedy got out the papers. Kearns filled them in for me. I signed them. Kearns took over the job of sending them in. They were never found.

With the end of the war I hoped the matter was ended. It wasn't, of course. It never will be, really, in my own heart.

The boys came marching home and the war was forgotten. But the crowds, they didn't forget me. I was booed when I fought Willard, though he seemed twice my size. I fought a Frenchman before an American audience and was booed. I fought an Argentinian before my countrymen and was booed.

I never had an "Aw, to hell with 'em— they paid their money" feeling about this contempt of some of my countrymen. It always dug deep and hurt terribly. I didn't think it was fair, because I never schemed or connived to avoid service. And it burned me further because I knew that many a guy booing me had a war record no more distinguished than my own poor thing.

The postwar newspapers generally confined their coverage of my life to my fights, those turkeys I made in Hollywood, an auto wreck now and then, and the girls I was supposed to be in love with. With one exception. The San Francisco sports editor never forgot.

His paper produced evidence that the government considered strong enough to bring charges against me for filing false claims about dependents. An American Legion post was behind the attack on me.

Jack during the First World War, at work in a shipyard.

Jack, on the left, and manager Jack Kearns.

In 1919 Jack (in the light trunks) beat Jess Willard in four rounds to become the heavyweight champion of the world.

Jack with his mother and father in 1920.

Jack and his first wife, Maxine.

Estelle Taylor, the movie star, married Jack in 1925.

Jack, on the right, in one of his many films.

That's Dempsey going out of the ring, in the famous fight with Luis Angel Firpo, the Wild Bull of the Pampas.

The champ in 1926.

Jack and the great Tex Rickard, who promoted the first million-dollar gate in history.

United Press International Photo

With Gene Tunney on the mat, the ref tries to get Jack to a neutral corner, but Dempsey is waiting for Tunney to stir—so he can hit him again. This was the beginning of the historic "long count."

In 1942 Jack enlisted in the Army and was rejected for being over age. He's shown here at the recruiting station.

The Coast Guard accepted Jack and made him director of their physical fitness program. He's landing on Okinawa a few hours after the initial attack.

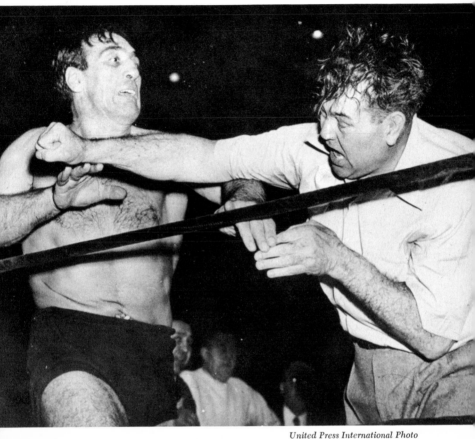

Jack, as referee, takes a swing at wrestler Primo Carnera after Carnera refused to heed his warnings to stop using rough tactics.

[OPPOSITE]
Jack's daughter Barbara (on the left) was 10 and Joan was 12 in 1947, when this picture was taken.

Hannah Williams was Jack's third wife and the mother of his children. This picture was taken in 1943, the year of their divorce.

Georges Carpentier, Luis Angel Firpo, and Jack, in a 1957 reunion of the three famous fighters, on "This Is Your Life."

Philippe Halsman

Jack Dempsey today.

And so was Maxine.

It was her testimony before a grand jury in March of 1920 that led to the indictment being handed down. Later she denied her charges in an affidavit. But early in June 1920 she stood in a San Francisco court and wept pathetically as she said I had never supported her as I claimed. I don't know why she cried. Nor why she lied. She didn't cry when the prosecution asked her to state her profession or when it was testified that she was a prostitute.

A prostitute is subject to many forms of intimidation. Maxine must have had them all.

To try to prove its point, the government introduced that silly shipyard picture and sent a parade of girls to the witness chair to admit they were prostitutes and to testify they had known me. As a friend, not a customer, they pointed out.

My mother and father testified that I supported them. Commander Kennedy, a handsome guy in uniform and with a hell of a war record, swore that I had made a serious effort to join the Navy.

I still don't know what my desire to join the Navy had to do with a charge of filing false claims for dependents. Or, for that matter, what the connection was between the charge and the fact that they said I was acquainted with a few prostitutes.

The trial lasted five days. They were the five saddest days of my life, and maybe the five saddest of Maxine's, and we had both known more than our share.

The jury was out for fifteen minutes. I was "Not Guilty."

It was a verdict that most people accepted, but not all. I still heard the word, from the middle of a row as I walked down the aisle toward a ring, or from out in left field after I was introduced. I can remember standing on a corner in New York with Estelle Taylor, just after we were married, and hearing a bum yell from a speeding car, "Hi, y' slacker!"

On vaudeville stages, after Kearns or some master of ceremonies had overintroduced me, I'd have trouble remembering what I had to say or do, because I was waiting for somebody out of reach to yell. Sometimes they gave me that word. Sometimes a guy would yell from the balcony, or from the back, "What about the patent-leather shoes, Champ?"

I'd go on with the show, and I'd feel better inside if the show had something to do with fighting. I think people came to see me fight at that time for two reasons. I usually gave them a hell of a show, and a certain portion of them hoped I'd give them a perfect evening's entertainment by getting knocked flat.

That portion of the public that wanted no part of me swung over in my favor the night I met Gene Tunney in the first of our two fights. Gene had a fine war record in the Marines, and yet all of a sudden I got as good a hand as he did. How do you figure out a thing like that? When I fought Jack Sharkey the following year I was fighting a veteran of the U.S. Navy. Yet everybody yelled for me before, during and after the fight.

Ever since that mysterious swing the American people have been wonderfully kind to me. Far kinder than any man deserves. I just don't know any words that can say how grateful I am for this. I thought many times it would never happen. But it did.

This is the first time I ever publicly discussed this subject. There is nothing more to be said except "Thanks," and "I was not a slacker."

CHAPTER **11**

MY FIRST DEFENSE OF THE TITLE WAS
on Labor Day, 1920, against a dying friend of mine. I
knocked him out because I loved the guy. Hell of a guy.
Billy Miske.

It happened in Benton Harbor. It was the third and last
time I fought Billy.

He was dying of Bright's disease. I didn't know it was

as bad as it was. All I knew was that he begged me for the fight. He was broke and needed a good payday so that he could rest and regain his health. There was never any question that it was a legitimate match. In one of our two previous fights he had held me to a draw and he had clouted me real good in the other.

You read a lot about "grudge matches," but there aren't really many. Of all the fights I had, as I said before, only the matches against Carl Morris had anything to do with bearing a grudge. Most fighters like each other. I guess the old gladiators felt the same way, even though one of them was going to die. Fighters know each other's problems, hopes, tough times. They feel for each other even as they bang away. Billy was my friend. He needed a payday.

People who don't fight are surprised when they hear of boxers going into the ring even if they're ill. I don't think there's a fighter alive today, or that one ever lived, who didn't battle at least once when he should have been in bed. I have, I know. Fighting's not much different from any other business. Everybody from the President on down has put in a day's or a week's work while sick. A boxer's work just happens to be fighting.

Kearns was feeling his oats and wouldn't do business with Rickard on this one. It was a day and age when fighters weren't tied up to promoters or corporations as they are today. Floyd Fitzsimmons promoted the Miske fight. But Kearns wanted to hammer him down to size too. He threatened to call the whole thing off twenty-four hours before Miske could make his buck, unless he could name his own referee— Jim Dougherty.

Kearns was a real ham, I was beginning to understand, but he was still the doctor. If he had told me to pack up and go home at that time, even though I felt for Miske, I would have obeyed him. Kearns was out to show the world, and especially Rickard, that he was a power, not just another towel swinger.

He got his way, not that it mattered any who was referee. So the fight went on.

There's been a story around for years that when I came into the ring and Miske looked at me, fit and ready, he lost control of himself. That's a damn lie. Billy was as brave as any fighter I ever met. No man who climbs through the ropes is a coward. There are just degrees of courage, and the men who are doing the fighting get the best view of these. You can respect a man who lasts maybe sixty wild seconds against you far more than you can respect a guy you chase for ten or fifteen rounds.

Now, the problem was how to handle Miske— carry him or put him out of his misery as soon as I could. If I carried him, I'd have to cut him up through the fight, to protect the title. And there is always a chance that he might connect, I'd get a bad cut and the fight might be stopped. If I tried for a kayo quick, I'd have it on my conscience.

I tried to knock him out in the first round, but the best I could do was hurt him with a body punch. I couldn't get a shot at his jaw. In the second round I got a part of it and knocked him down. In the third round I just shut my eyes, hit him with a left that straightened him up, then let the right hand go— and that's all there was to it.

I carried Billy to his stool and nearly got sick to my

stomach while the two seconds worked on him bringing him to. I had forgotten the boos before the fight and now I couldn't hear the cheers for me, cheers that always came after winning one. The crowd was very excited, and as a matter of fact it had been an exciting fight.

Suddenly, and for the first time in my fight life, I hated those guys who were cheering for me. Billy Miske, my friend, was still out. It was the only time in my life I was ashamed of being a fighter.

Kearns and I split $55,000, the biggest touch we had ever had. It wasn't enough for such filthy work. The only good feeling I had about the fight was that Billy got his payday, about $25,000 which was double or triple the best purse he had ever had. Or ever would. He didn't live long after that.

He was such a fine guy. I hope the payday helped through those last weeks.

Bill Brennan was next. The second time around. Old Madison Square Garden. It was December 1920. The newspapers had an angle they kept stressing: if Brennan hadn't broken his ankle in the first fight, he might have won.

I trained on the *Granite State*, a ship docked at Ninety-sixth Street. I brought myself around to perfect shape. Then the fight was postponed for three weeks. I went as stale as if I was a piece of bread, for I kept training, trying to stay in the pink.

We drew a full house, and a lot of them gave me a hard time when I was introduced. But not as hard a time as

Brennan was going to give me. In the second, Bill hit me a right on the chin that made me stagger around, looking for my corner, at the end of the round. The only memory I have of the five or six rounds that followed are of Kearns screaming into my ear while he worked on me, "He's licking you, Jack. You're gonna blow the title."

I was just coming out of the haze in the ninth when Bill reached down and hit me with a chopping right that cut me all along where my ear joined my head. I had been fighting in a crouch. Bill was a stand-up fighter. Suddenly the whole side of my head was warm with my blood. I touched my ear and it felt like it was hanging off, like a busted awning.

I felt almost the same kind of fear as I did the night John Lester Johnson caved in my ribs. I was afraid that if Bill hit me a solid punch, or even a grazing one, he might knock the ear off. I was afraid of losing my title, too, losing it in the first real test I had had.

You can do some strange things when you're desperate. My corner did a good job patching me up before the tenth. I got through that round all right. My head was clear now. In the eleventh I went out to get him or be gotten. For the first time in the fight I nailed him pretty good, a body punch. But Bill had a lot left. He was as confident that he could beat me as he had been four years before, when I was his fifty-cents-a-day sparring partner. By the end of the eleventh, he had taken charge of me again, moving me around, poking me.

In my corner after the eleventh, they told me something

that wasn't news. They told me that I had to knock him out to win.

I went out there swinging for his jaw, but Bill was too smart for me. I went for his body with everything I had. I dug a right into his solar plexus up to my wrist and when he doubled over I got him on the ribs with a left hook that had everything I owned.

Brennan dropped. He was hurt and there wasn't any wind in him. But he started up. I charged him, but the referee, who had been standing over him, stepped between us. The fight was over. I couldn't believe it, and a lot of people in the crowd couldn't either. An announcement had to be made. The referee said he hadn't stopped it because of Brennan's condition but because Bill's knee was still on the canvas when he called ten.

A close one.

Brennan came in to see them hemstitch my ear back on. He was laughing.

"It took you twice as long this time, you lucky stiff," he said as we shook hands. "It's my turn next. Out you go."

Bill meant it, too. It would have been a great return match. But the only time we came close to getting into the same ring for a third fight was when we were matched to fight in Michigan City a year or so after this one. The governor of Michigan stopped that one. There was some trouble on the old slacker charge.

Brennan took the money he had made out of the Garden match and opened a speakeasy. One night a couple of tough guys walked in and told him he was buying the

wrong mob's beer. Bill had the guts of a lion. He threw
them both out, himself. A few nights later he was sitting
with some friends, having a nice time, when word came
that there was a fellow at the door who wanted to see him.

Bill went to the door. A guy he had never seen before
was waiting for him. The guy pulled a gun and killed Bill.

Bill bought the wrong beer.

The Brennan fight had been the biggest touch Kearns
and I had made. Our end came to $100,000, plus $8,000
for the movies. Minus expenses, of course.

It was a real bundle, but just the beginning. The Carpentier fight was in the works.

I'm leveling when I tell you that it was probably the
worst mismatch in the history of the heavyweight division.
Yet it became the first fight ever to do a million dollars—
the gross was $1,626,580— and the first fight ever to draw
anywhere near the 91,000 fans who showed up to see it.
July 2, 1921. Boyle's Thirty Acres, New Jersey.

No fight, but *no* fight, ever had a build-up like this one.
The contracts were signed in November 1920, a month
before I fought Brennan in the Garden. But the steam was
in the boiler before that. As early as March 1920, after my
indictment and before the trial, Carpentier's manager,
Deschamps, released a story to the papers saying his fighter, the European champion, wouldn't meet me until
"Dempsey's military affairs are cleared up."

From then on until we stepped into the ring and squared
off, the Frenchman was the hero and I was the flat-nosed
bum. His military record was built up until it sounded like

he won the war. Mine was written as if I had almost caused our side to lose it. He had courage, I lacked guts. He had fought them all, from the flyweight division right up. I was an untested, lucky stiff.

Georges was a beautiful-looking guy. Still is, for that matter. But back in May 1921, when I first saw him, he was really something to look at. It was no wonder that for probably the first time since fist fighting began women were buying tickets or asking to be taken to the fight.

We met first on a golf course, of all places. Bob Edgren, who could write and draw sports as good as anybody who ever lived, invited me out to a course in New Jersey to play with Carpentier. I didn't want to go— I wasn't a golfer— but it turned out that Carpentier had accepted, and Edgren was a nice guy, so there I was on the first tee with one of those shinny sticks in my hand.

He was a good golfer, which didn't surprise me. What did surprise me was that he spoke good English and that he looked skinny. He had more charm, more good manners, and more class in his dress than anybody I had ever met. But he was frail-looking and— well, I thought of him as anything except a fighter. It was just that I didn't understand good manners much.

When we had finished our round and got back to the locker room Carpentier smiled at me and said, "Jack, when our fight is done I hope we will still be such good friends."

I mumbled something like "I hope so too."

We had worked up a mild sweat hacking around the course. Carpentier stripped down for a shower, and for the first time I could understand how he had knocked out some of those guys overseas. He had tremendous arms and legs, the sign of a puncher.

But he wasn't a heavyweight any more than I was King Tut.

That's why Georges worked and trained in secret. If the boxing writers had seen him, fast and skillful as he was they'd have laughed the match out of existence. But none of them really saw much of him.

After Ring Lardner had been turned away from Carpentier's camp in Great Neck, Long Island, for the third time on the grounds that the Frenchman was "sleeping," he went home and wrote a story saying "Carpentier is practicing ten-second naps." Most of the others kept writing about what a war hero he was, and what a right hand he had.

Kearns was busy trying not to show how confident he was that I'd win. He kept telling me, "You'll kill him, Jack. He's just a bum."

He was busy blowing one, too. A week before the fight he went to Rickard and changed the contract. We had signed for $300,000 or 50 per cent. Doc waived the 50 per cent. "Just give us the three hundred thousand and we'll be happy," he said. Rickard was happy to oblige.

It didn't mean much to me when he told me. Three hundred thousand was all the money in the world, after what I had been through.

As it turned out, Kearns's decision cost us $150,000. The crowd started coming when the sun came up July 2, and they were still coming when the fight started that afternoon.

It started sooner than I expected. It was scheduled for

three or three-thirty, but at one o'clock that afternoon the chief of police and the fire chief of Harrison, New Jersey, came to the place where I was staying.

"Come on," one of them said. "Rickard's waiting for you. Lots of trouble. Looks like the arena's going to fall down. The damn thing is full of people and it's beginning to sway back and forth. Rickard wants to put the fight on before it falls and hurts a lot of people."

Rickard was standing in my dressing-room door, stamping his cane and chewing his cigar, when I arrived. He was very excited.

"Jack," he said, "you never seed anything like it. We got a million dollars in already, and they're still coming. And the people, Jack! I never seed anything like the people we got, at a fight. High-class society folks. And dames. I mean classy dames. Thousands of them."

Then he calmed down. "Jack," he said, taking me inside. "This is the biggest day the boxing business ever had. I don't want you messing it up. This is just the beginning. We'll be drawing millions more before this is over."

I was in good shape, so I was nervous and rude, even to this man I liked so much. "I ain't gonna mess nothin' up, Tex," I said to him, hot like. "Just tell that frog not to run, and I'll give you a good fight."

Tex came to the point. "Don't kill him, Jack," he said seriously. "If you kill him you kill boxing."

I told you Tex was a peculiar man. Whenever he was stuck on a fighter, as he was on me and had been on Willard and Johnson, he thought the fighter might kill somebody.

"I just want you to knock him out, that's all," he said.

"Not with a punch or in the first round. Give them a run for their money."

It isn't true— as was written for so many years later— that Tex asked me to carry Carpentier "for the pictures."

When he had finished, that day in my dressing room, I said to him, "Tex, this guy is going out as soon as I can take him. I'm not carrying nobody for nobody, even for you."

No matter what has been written, I didn't carry Carpentier for one second. He went as soon as I could arrange it.

We came to our corners at the same time. There had never been a crowd like it anywhere. Arthur Brisbane, who said a gorilla could lick us both, wrote that it was like a big saucer of honey filled with flies.

There were some people there who didn't like me. The first thing I heard when I climbed into the ring and dug my shoes into the resin was a guy with a bull voice who cut through the crowd noises and yelled, "You bum, I hope you get killed." Others yelled, "Slacker."

Deschamps came to my corner as I was getting ready. He tried to hypnotize me. I laughed at him. Nobody could do a thing like that.

The champion is always introduced first. Joe Humphreys, the greatest of fight announcers, a guy who didn't need a microphone, picked up his megaphone and, turning slowly, bawled, "In this corner, weighing one hundred and eighty-eight pounds, from Salt Lake City, Utah, the heavyweight champion of the world— Jack Dempsey."

There isn't anything much more American than Salt

Lake City, Utah. But the only response from ninety-one thousand Americans was a little applause and a low murmur. It hurt, believe me.

Now Joe belted out the rest of his bit. "And in this corner, weighing one hundred and seventy-five pounds, the challenger from Paris, France— Georges Carpentier."

The people went wild. It was deafening.

The first round wasn't much. I was feeling the guy out. There were some boos for me.

He hit me with a real good right in the second. Jimmy Johnston, who saw them all, used to say that Carpentier had the best right hand of all. I don't know. But it was a hell of a right. It was sneaky, too, and he could deliver it after or during the midst of a lot of those funny springs and lunges that the European fighters go in for. It landed high on my left cheekbone. If he had hit me on the chin there's a good chance he would have knocked me down, and a fair chance he would have knocked me out.

It was a good punch, but it wasn't in the right place. He followed it up, like the pro he was. He bounced five in a row off my head before I could hit him. I busted him a right in the mouth and I knew I had him licked. He hadn't hurt me, and I could see he wouldn't be able to take my punch.

In the third I concentrated on getting him to bring his guard down. I concentrated on his body. In the fourth I nailed him with a left hook and he went down for nine. He got up, groggy. Another left sent him down, and while he was falling I nailed him with a right. Time: fifty-seven seconds of the fourth round.

He couldn't have weighed more than 168 or 170.

I read the stories about the fight in the next day's papers and felt that I hadn't won. Carpentier was the hero of the hour. Never before had anybody seen such courage. I was just a butcher who had happened to win.

Georges *had* shown all the courage any man could have shown under the circumstances. He had fought until unconscious. That's all you can ask of anybody.

But I was a pretty bitter fellow. No matter what you've got, you want them to like you.

CHAPTER **12**

THE ONLY FIGHTING I DID IN 1922 WAS
exhibition work. I showed five times— against fighters like
Jack Renault— for spending money. The rest of the year
was for laughs.

In the spring of that year a bunch of us went to
Europe. We really had a ball. There were Kearns, Joe

Benjamin and Teddy Hayes. I guess there haven't been many guys who were more ready for anything than those three. Or me. We took along Jimmy Hussey, an actor and writer and a real clever guy. And Damon Runyon went for the Hearst papers and his syndicate.

We just had a good time— lots of cafés, dancing, going to the race tracks, receptions and laughs. It couldn't happen nowadays. For instance, we had a big party on the *Aquitania* before we left and newspapers actually carried interviews with three girls who were there— Mary Lewis of the *Follies*, Florence Walton, the dancer, and Mary Sherman, who was in the movies— discussing how it was to kiss me. Must have gotten quite a laugh in a lot of jungles along the tracks of the West.

I met nobility and wondered how the boys back in Provo and Montrose would take it. I met the prince who later became king. He was as shy and as embarrassed about talking as I had been, and yet he was to become a great king.

The big highlight of the trip was a lunch given for me by Lord Northcliffe, the British publisher, at his town house. I bought a cutaway coat and striped pants and looked like a real dude by the time I was ready to leave the hotel for the party.

Kearns and the others were still in the sack, after a hard night. But Runyon was up and dressed.

"I'm going with you," he said.

"I thought you said you weren't invited."

"I wasn't," he said, "but I'm going with you."

I didn't know what to do for a minute. Then I said,

"They don't do things like that over here, Damon. It's a private party. If you want to go, go ahead. But I'm not inviting you."

I went alone and soon found myself mingling with generals, lords, and dukes. I don't think any fighter was ever treated better than I was that day by Englishmen who probably had trouble understanding the way I used their language. At lunch I didn't know whether to use a knife or a fork, but I'd wait and watch, and if they noticed they didn't let on.

Right in the middle of lunch a butler came to Lord Northcliffe and gave him a calling card. Northcliffe got up from the table and went to the door.

I couldn't help hearing the conversation.

"I'm Damon Runyon. I'm covering Jack Dempsey's trip abroad and I'd like to take in this luncheon."

There was a pause, during which I guess Northcliffe looked at our great sports writer like he was a roach or something.

"I'm very sorry," I could hear him say, "but this is a private party for Mr. Dempsey. Good afternoon."

Damon never got over it. He had known me when I was a bum.

Paris was better. It was more in tune with our crowd. More girls. More action. A lot of crazy, wonderful things happened. The reception committee showed up at the railroad station twenty-four hours late. The most I did with Peggy Hopkins Joyce, who was there at the time, was shake hands, but when she sailed a few days later the papers said she nearly drowned in tears of disappointment because I didn't see her off. The French government gave me a medal and *l'Echo de Sport* threw me a big banquet, just like I had never beaten their big hero, Carpentier.

I went to the races at Longchamps, gave a formal party at Ciro's for Fanny Ward. There were things to do every night, and we did every single one of them. One night at a joint where Tommy Lyman was playing they talked me into an exhibition dance with Yancsi Dolly. Irving Berlin played for us. It must have been a slaughter.

There had been a little talk about a return match with Carpentier, for Paris. But they had seen the pictures. The only time I came close to a ring was one night I refereed a fight, sitting in a comfortable chair and wearing a tux— or dinner jacket, as Georges taught me to call it. He had also taught me just enough French so that I could announce the decision.

There wasn't much doubt in my mind who the winner would be. When the fight ended, I climbed into the ring, held up the hand of a guy named Billy Balzac and yelled, "*Le victor,* Monsewer Billy Balzac."

I wasn't sure he won or not. But there wasn't much I could do. The other guy's name was Maurice Prunier or Proxineaux or something like that. How the hell could I have given it to him?

Georges joined me in the ring and put his arm around my shoulders. "Jack," he said, rubbing his jaw, "if you had a right hand like your French accent I'd be heavyweight champion of the world."

The European trip was coming to an end. We all wanted to see Berlin, and did, and might have stayed longer. But the dogs drove us out. The Berlin boxing fans helped, too. They tore half my clothes off the first day we were there. But it was the dogs that clinched it.

I told the German reporters how crazy I had always been about dogs, that the German shepherd was my favorite dog, that I had some back home, and that more than anything else I wanted to buy one while in Berlin. The next day about five thousand owners of German shepherds almost did to the Adlon Hotel what our bombers did years later in World War II. Wreck it. They came from all sections of the city and maybe from all corners of Germany. The grounds and lobby and hallways of the Adlon looked like the biggest dog show you ever saw, with only one kind of dog on display.

We had to blow town, but that wasn't hard. To get to the boat, a fellow had to go back through Paris.

Paris was always quite a town and always will be. But you should've seen it, and its girls, in 1922— especially if you could have been my age and heavyweight champion of the world.

Kearns put me to work right after we got back, to pay for the trip. He found tame ones for me in Canada, Boston and Michigan City. I knocked out three of them in one round one night in Montreal. But this wasn't what the public wanted and Kearns knew it. He kept looking and looking, figuring where the best buck was, and early in

1923 he came up with a fight that couldn't take place today— my fight with Tommy Gibbons in Shelby, Montana.

The fight itself was the least part of that one.

The first thing I said to Kearns when he told me he had
lined me up to fight Gibbons at Shelby was, "I never heard
of it."

"It ain't a big place," Doc said, "but the money's there.
Some oil fellows out there want to put the town on the
map, sell some oil stocks."

"I don't want to fight in no place named Shelby, Doc.
It's crazy."

"They're going to give us two-fifty and fifty per cent,"
he said.

"Well, okay," I said. "But I'm going to hold you responsible for the money."

I was growing up, I guess.

It was the most fouled-up promotion of my boxing life.
Kearns didn't even talk about the fight with Rickard, the
man who had made us the most money of our lives. But
that wasn't too unusual in those days. Promoters seldom if
ever had exclusive rights to a fighter, such as Mike Jacobs
had years later with Joe Louis and I.B.C. had with
others. I never had a contract with Rickard. I never had a
contract with Kearns.

We got $100,000 on signing. The contract called for
another $100,000 thirty days before the fight. But the oil
stock hustlers and the honest slobs of Shelby who were
now pulled into the deal just couldn't get up the second
payment.

I was tough. "Where's the money?" I asked Kearns.

"Now, don't you worry, boy—" he started. He should have sold oil stocks himself.

"Doc," I said, "I told you if they don't get the money up I'm not going to fight."

"I'll get it. You can count on me."

I was beginning to wonder just how much I *could* count on Doc. I got Rickard on the phone and told him what was happening. Without hesitating a minute, Rickard said he'd get hold of the promoters, Kearns, Gibbons and everybody else concerned, and if it was acceptable to them he'd move the whole fight to New York, see that everybody got paid what he was promised. Tex was a big-league fellow.

It sounded great to me, but not to Shelby. They had booked a fight and, by God, they were going to hold one. The promoters tapped the local American Legion treasury for money, put the arm on the storekeepers again and got up the second $100,000. We were going to fight in Shelby, they said, or we weren't ever going to fight anywhere else. Maybe they were kidding, maybe not. They were desperate.

The last $50,000 was supposed to be paid ten days before the fight, but there wasn't a quarter left in town or anywhere in that whole area. Kearns waived the ten-day clause on the final payment. He told them we'd take it out of the gate. We never got it all. The amazing thing is that we got what we did and got out of town.

There was so little order around the arena on the day of the fight that half the crowd of eight thousand must have pushed by the gates and gotten in free. It was the roughest crowd I ever fought in front of, that's for sure. There were guns, whisky bottles and lariats. During the preliminaries guys lassoed the fences, pulled them down, and many got in for nothing.

For the first and only time, I was more worried about getting hurt by the crowd than by the guy I was fighting. I got a pretty good blast when introduced. The crowd was hollering and raising hell. I looked around for my body-guard, a colorful New York character named Wild Bill Lyons, who packed two pearl-handled pistols and used to talk a lot about his days in the West. Wild Bill was under the ring, hiding.

Tommy was a much better fighter than most people thought he was. He had his mind made up that he could stay away from my punches and win the decision. He knew I hadn't fought anybody since Carpentier two years before, and even that wasn't much of a fight. What he didn't know was that I wasn't in the shape I should've been in. I was nearly knocked out twice training in Great Falls.

Every time he touched me, or I missed with a hard one, the crowd whooped and hollered for Tommy. I thought I was winning, but you'd never know it from the sound of the crowd.

Then something happened in the seventh. The crowd seemed to understand all at once that I wasn't carrying him, that I was trying to make a fight out of it and that all he wanted to do was stab and run. They swung to me. It went the full fifteen rounds. Nailing him was like trying to thread a needle in a high wind.

We were packed and ready to go, and we got out of town as quickly and as quietly as we could. I don't know what would have happened if we had hung around until the promoters started remembering that we were the only ones who made money off the fight.

Poor Tommy didn't get a quarter. He had said so often, "I'll fight Dempsey for nothing," and that's just what they gave him.

It got him seven or eight weeks on the Pantages circuit.

It's a good thing I fought Gibbons, because it put me in shape. If I had fought Firpo in the same shape I was in when I met Tommy, I'd have been knocked out for sure.

I didn't know much about Firpo except that he had beat up some guys I never heard of in South America and then he came up here and knocked out Willard in six. In my mind, he was just a big, clumsy ox.

"You watch this guy," Rickard told me after we had signed. "He's a good fighter, good right-hand puncher." But I still didn't think he could fight a hell of a lot.

I sure underestimated Luis.

They're still talking about the Firpo fight, and I guess they always will.

When the introductions and the boos were over that night in September 1923 at the jam-packed Polo Grounds, I went across the ring after the big fellow as fast as I could move. I jabbed him, hit him with a kind of sounding-out left. Then I missed a right.

I reared back and, just as I did, he caught me with a

right hand on my cheekbone. If I hadn't been going away it would have knocked me cold. Flat on my back. As it was, it knocked me out on my feet.

If you've seen the movies of the fight, you know what happened the rest of the round. Seeing the pictures the day after the fight was the only way *I* ever learned about what happened.

I knocked him down six or seven times. I hit him a couple times before he got off the floor. I stepped over him a couple of times. I didn't know what I was doing. I was dazed and out on my feet.

I have no memory to this day of the most spectacular thing that ever happened to me in my fighting life— being knocked out of the ring by Firpo.

There was just this fog in front of my eyes, and through it I could see this big guy getting up every time I knocked him down, and the crowd was screaming so loud it made it even harder for my brain to try to think. It was still the first round.

Then he was up again and on me like a giant. He outweighed me forty pounds. I backed up as he came on, trading punches. I was instinctively waiting for my back to touch the ropes, I guess. But just before I could touch, and with about ten seconds left of the first round, he half hit and half shoved me with a right to the face.

I went out of the ring backward, between the top and middle ropes, and landed on my neck on Jack Lawrence's typewriter in the first row of the press section.

I don't remember getting back into the ring. The first clear thing was that I was sitting on my stool and the three guys in my corner— Kearns, Benjamin and Jerry the Greek

— were cursing one another. They couldn't find the smelling salts, that's what the argument was about. Finally Kearns found the bottle in his shirt pocket and pushed it under my nose. They slapped me a lot.

"What round was I knocked out in?" I said.

They were rubbing my back and arms now.

"You just slipped," Kearns said. "You're coming out for the second." My head was now clear and I could think.

I went out after him again, but this time with respect. I wasn't going to get nailed again. I stuck a right under his left hand and finally crossed him on the chin. He was swaying like a ship at sea. Two good lefts to the jaw, and that was all there was to it.

Kearns and I were growing further apart. He was in to me for some money I had put up to buy some California property which was in both our names. I had a feeling that unless I could get my hands on the money out of the Firpo fight, I wouldn't see what he owed me for a long time.

I told Rickard that this time I would take charge of the money and split it with Doc. That was okay with Rickard, so bright and early the morning after the Firpo fight I went to Rickard's office and he had it waiting for me. It was a real bundle for a former bindle stiff — $500,000.

Kearns couldn't get to Rickard's office that day. When he showed up the next day, there was no money there, of course. Rickard told me what happened.

"I gave it to Jack," Tex said.

"Well, damn you," Kearns said, moving at him. "I'm the manager! You should've given it to me."

Kearns was just as sore at me as he was at Tex.

"You got that money?" he said when he came into my hotel room.

"Yeah." I wasn't going to get excited. I counted out what was coming to him and took what he owed me. This time I got more than he did, and it burned him.

"What the hell you going to do with that money?" he yelled at me.

"Well, I'm putting two hundred thousand in a trust fund," I said.

"What interest?"

"I dunno. Three-four-five per cent, whatever I'm going to get."

Doc looked at me like I was dirt.

"You damn fool," he said, shaking his head, "I could get you fifteen per cent."

I had to say it then, or maybe never.

"Doc," I said, "I'm going to put that money where I know I'll have it when I'm old."

He blew. Hot as hell.

CHAPTER **13**

THE TITLE DIDN'T CHANGE ONLY MY
own life. It changed the lives of people around me. People
I loved, like my mother. People I had begun growing
away from, like Kearns. I think it indirectly killed my
brother Johnny, too.

Los Angeles became my base, mainly because the money

—the nonfight money—was there. Over the years, L.A. has been easily the most important city in my life. Right now everything that really means anything to me is in that city— my daughters Barbara and Joan and their wonderful families. They have been the only true, constant happiness of my life.

But Los Angeles held most of the sorrow of my adult life, too. It was there I flunked, trying to hold the love of a wife I loved very much. It was in L.A. also that I ended my life with another wife I loved by a sensational and unpleasant divorce action. And in Los Angeles I watched helplessly as Johnny, happy and handsome Johnny, slowly but surely ground himself into the destruction of a dope fiend.

I had my most serious trouble and final showdown with Kearns in Los Angeles.

Funny thing about L.A., I was a mighty proud and happy guy when I led the family out there. I thought I was doing everybody a favor, mostly my mother. Buying homes for my mother had become the biggest kick I got out of spending my ring money. First there was the little place I got her with the Fulton money. Later I bought her a nice place on Center Street, "up on the hill," in Salt Lake City. Then one in a pretty fashionable neighborhood on East South Temple Street. This, I thought, was it. My mother had been a gypsy most of her life and had worked so terribly hard. Now she had this place and I hired enough servants to run it for her.

They made her nervous. She was lonely. So I got a great idea.

"Mom, why don't you and Elsie move to Los Angeles?" I suggested. "You'll have a home in a nice warm city and I can live right there with you. I'll make it my base." She nodded, and I guess she must have sighed.

But I didn't see anything except the nod. I went out and bought a $75,000 home for her at Twenty-fourth and Western Avenue.

My mother was pleased enough about making a home for me and the others. But without realizing it I was subjecting her to the same kind of torture my father had put her through. I had given her everything except the one big thing she wanted, a nice little farm among her beloved Mormons. Still, the sense of duty and love that made her follow my wandering old man made her follow her wandering son Harry.

This was 1923, a wild and carefree time in Los Angeles. My mother was hard for a lot of my fair-weather friends to understand. She could have slept until noon if she'd wanted, and had her breakfast served by a French maid. But she was up at six and in bed by ten. She insisted upon grace being offered at every meal even with bums at the table who thought grace was some babe and God a cuss word. She didn't like smoking and she hated drinking. She meant it when she prayed and when she went to church.

My mother kept the place on Western Avenue spotless, except for the people who began coming there soon after we got settled. It became an all-night restaurant. I hired a special short-order cook to handle the food orders of people who dropped in after the shows or the fights. You know, actors, actresses, sports writers and characters. My mother wondered. I tried to explain that a champ had to live like a champ. He doesn't, of course. But Kearns had sold me on the value of ballyhoo— that if I didn't have people like this on my side I was nothing. My mother wasn't convinced.

"Harry," she'd say, "why don't they go home when you go to bed? You always say, 'Well, fellows, I'm kinda tired, but you stick around as long as you like.' Then they stay until the sun's up."

She took it for a year and then started packing. I got her a twenty-two-acre farm outside Salt Lake City. I saw to it that my father was living comfortably, in town.

But I kept the house in Los Angeles. I had just met Estelle Taylor and I wanted to be near her. There was no connection between my mother's return to Utah and the fact that Miss Taylor had come into my life. My mother liked her very much. Matter of fact, she also liked the wife that followed Miss Taylor, Hannah Williams.

Miss Taylor and I were married in 1925 in San Diego in a quiet little wedding. There couldn't have been more than fifty friends, relatives, reporters and photographers.

She was more than a beautiful movie star. She had wit, a fast mind and a sense of humor like a razor. Her friends were bright, sometimes brilliant, people. She put me into another world. I tried like the devil to fit and couldn't. Sometimes it was a little lonely being there. They talked over my head a lot. No snubs, really. Nobody snubs the heavyweight champion of the world. It was just that I'd get a feeling now and then that I didn't know what the hell they were talking about. It wasn't much comfort to tell myself that maybe they didn't either.

Miss Taylor's career began going badly right after we were married. She wasn't a great actress. Her only real weapon was her great beauty. I guess everybody looks around for somebody to blame his failures on, and I was her nearest target. It began to be my fault if she didn't get a part. She explained to me that social contacts play an important role in the success or failure of Hollywood stars, and being married to a pug hurt her socially and therefore hurt her career.

Then there was Kearns. He was no help. Miss Taylor would have nothing to do with Kearns. Kearns felt the same way toward her. This didn't break up our marriage later, as many have written. I kept Kearns away from her when he and I were doing business, and we parted company not too long after Miss Taylor and I got married.

But in the seven years we were married there were many happy moments, lots of love, and lots of laughs. She called me Ginsberg.

Miss Taylor and I had one great interest in common: we both loved dogs.

When I was a kid in Utah and Colorado there were always dogs around the house, sometimes bloodhounds and staghounds to keep the coyotes away from the stock, sometimes bird dogs to help us get our food. There were always dogs around my fight camps. I bred dogs. I trained and pitted dogs. When I was getting ready for Gibbons at my Great Falls, Montana, camp my closest friend was White

Wolf, a one-man dog I bred by mating a wolf to a black German shepherd bitch. White Wolf was the only pup born of the mating and he was a brute. You had to make him know who was boss or he'd kill you. Frankly, that was the kind of dog I liked best— an ornery half-wolf or a courageous pit-fighting bulldog. Every time I got mixed up with a pet-type dog there was hell to pay.

Let me tell you about Castor. You had to be a real dog lover to love Castor.

Miss Taylor and I went to Europe right after our marriage. It was a combined honeymoon and gold-hunting trip. The gold was there, too. The pickings were best in Luna Park, Berlin, where I got $1,000 a night for taking on from three to five hopefuls who had traveled to Berlin from all over Europe for a shot at my chin. (Some of them were pros who took fake names and forged amateur "records" just to take that do-or-die shot.) It was 1926 and the German mark had blown sky-high, so I insisted on being paid each night. Figuring out what those millions of marks they gave me meant in dollars was a lot tougher than taking on the hopefuls.

Anyway, one afternoon I took a call at the Adlon from an old English fighter. The fellow had settled in Berlin and gone into the dog business. He had a dog he wanted to show me. I like old fighters almost as much as I like dogs, so I invited him over.

He walked into our suite with the biggest damn dog I ever saw, maybe the biggest dog anybody ever saw. He was a slate-gray animal nine months old. He weighed 210 pounds, twenty pounds more than I did and about a hundred pounds more than Miss Taylor.

"This is Castor," the old fighter said. I was afraid to shake hands with him.

Castor was a Bismarck. A Bismarck is something like a great Dane, only bigger. Not many people own Bismarcks. I can understand why. The old fighter couldn't do much more than introduce us. He was trying to keep from being pulled off his feet by Castor.

"Thanks, pardner," I said, "but no. If I want a horse I'll buy a horse."

That would have been that, but unfortunately Miss Taylor was in the room and she thought Castor was cute. She put her arms around his big neck and talked to this monster like a puppy. Castor liked Miss Taylor too. What could I do? I knew I'd blow the decision but I gave it a try.

"Honey," I said, "this thing weighs more than I do." Castor thought it was a compliment or something. He came over to me, reared up and put his front paws on my shoulders. "And, besides, the dog is a foot taller than I am, too."

I went for $250 for Castor. Without Miss Taylor ohing and ahing and talking baby talk, I could've gotten him for a double sawbuck.

But I got around to liking Castor a lot. He was friendly and remarkably smart. So we decided to take him to Luna Park with us the night after we bought him. I put Lee Moore in charge of the big chain we held him with. Lee was nearer Castor's weight than I was.

Well, I had just collected my suitcase of marks, and Miss Taylor, Lee, Castor and I were standing at the top of a flight of steps in the park saying good night, when suddenly I heard a woman at the bottom of the steps yell something that sounded like "Castor. Here, Castor!"

Castor lit out like a rocket. Lee had wrapped the chain around his wrist, and he took off like something being towed through the air. The first step he hit was halfway down the flight of stairs. He bumped and bounced the rest of the way. Castor dragged him right up to the woman and began licking her face.

There was a lot of yelling. The woman, a German, claimed she was Castor's original owner. She had asked the old English fighter to try to sell him for her. She was overjoyed when he came back to her without Castor and gave her the $50 he said I had paid for the monster. It was double what she expected.

Then she read in the Berlin papers that I had paid $250.

She kept yelling that I had robbed her of her dog, that I had stolen it. There must have been a couple of hundred people around us now, and the cops were showing up from all sides. Estelle got a word in at the top of her lungs. She said Castor didn't belong to either the woman or to me. Castor was hers.

The cops said "Let's go," in German, and we all wound up in the police station. But after a couple of hours the desk sergeant, or whatever he was, ruled that our purchase papers on Castor were okay and that the big mutt was really ours.

We all went wearily back to the Adlon, Castor wagging his baseball-bat-size tail happily.

In the middle of the night the telephone rang. Miss Taylor answered it. A clerk said to her, "Mrs. Dempsey, the police are here for the *hund*." The German woman had gotten a court order.

Miss Taylor went into hysterics.

"Please don't let them take my darling dog," she screamed at me, like the heroine of a bad movie. "I love him, Jack. I love him madly. Save him. We'll never see him again if that awful woman gets her hands on him."

So I grabbed Castor and ran him up a flight of stairs to the eighth floor. Doc Myers, a friend of mine who had come along for the ride, had a room up there above our suite.

Castor and I burst into his room and I said, "Doc, the cops are after this big dog. Hide him."

Doc said, "How the hell could you hide something like that?"

I put the end of the chain in his hand, beat it out of there, bounded down the steps, and got to the front door of our suite just as the cops got off the elevator.

"We got rid of the dog," I said. "Too much trouble. Come in and look around."

They came in and looked around but weren't very convinced until I gave them a couple of cigars. Then they went away.

Miss Taylor was very grateful. I put out my arms. "Go get him," she said. "I miss him."

As I started up the steps to the eighth floor again I could see Castor and Doc in the hall outside his room. So I called to him softly, "Here, Castor. Here, boy."

Doc took off in the air behind Castor. He bounced once or twice in the hall and then hit every step on the way

DEMPSEY *by the Man Himself*

down. He too had made the mistake of wrapping the chain around his wrist to get a better hold.

I got Castor free of Doc, who was on the floor moaning, and took him in to Miss Taylor, who kissed him. Then I went back to see about Doc.

"I'm bleedin' like a pig, Jack," he said. "That damn horse of yours busted every stitch in my guts."

So while Miss Taylor happily hugged the new love of her life, I called an ambulance and got Doc to the nearest hospital for some emergency resewing.

We had to leave Berlin for Paris. Smuggling Castor out was going to take some doing. Miss Taylor demanded that nothing go wrong, and I was all for that, too. Life without Castor would be worse than life with Castor.

So I called my trainer, Gus Wilson, who could speak German, and outlined my plot. "You take all our baggage, Gus," I said, "and get half a dozen guys to carry it and form a circle around Castor. That way nobody will see him until he's in our compartment."

Miss Taylor and I watched Gus shape up his troops, put Castor in the middle of them and start across the concourse of the big, crowded station. We followed the group. Nobody, not even the sharpest-eyed cop, would know there was a 210-pound dog in the middle of that pack ahead of us.

I beamed down at Miss Taylor and winked. The old Manassa Mauler wasn't all muscle. The boy could think pretty good, too. Miss Taylor looked up at me adoringly with those big dark eyes. At that moment, I'd say, she loved me almost as much as she loved Castor.

It was too good to be true.

In Paris Castor caused a lot of people to run for cover, but the French cops were easier to take care of than the German ones. So it was a pretty peaceful trip and stayed that way until we got to the ship at Cherbourg. Castor got seasick walking up the gangplank and was sick enough to die all the way across the Atlantic.

When we got to New York we took the poor, weak thing to the Hotel Alamac and called for a vet. The dog doctor was startled to see Castor but went to work on him and after a long study recommended something I didn't think Castor would ever need again, a laxative.

Nothing happened.

That night we moved on to Chicago. There was no cab big enough to hold Castor. I hired an open-air car and got him in the back seat. Miss Taylor waved to us as she left in her cab. Castor and the heavyweight champion of the world pulled up to the Morrison Hotel in a creaking old open-air hack.

The Morrison had a revolving door. Castor was much too big to fit into a partition. So I boosted him up on his hind feet and walked him in the semicircle from the street to the lobby.

The experience frightened Castor. Soon as we were in the lobby he jerked free of me. Before I could recapture him, the bill for damages was $500.

On to California.

Trying for a little privacy, Miss Taylor and I rented a swell little home in the hills of Hollywood. All was quiet and peaceful. Then, the second day we were there, an Airedale came over and picked a fight with Castor. Castor killed the game little dog.

Turned out that the Airedale's owner, who hated actresses and prize fighters and was our landlord, a bad combination, called the police and yelled, "That man has a wild dog."

So once again we had the problem of hiding Castor. This time we hid him in the trunk room, where he lay nice and quiet while I persuaded the friendly cops that we wouldn't think of keeping a dog.

The entire house had been beautifully and expensively furnished before we rented. Our bedroom was something I couldn't have even dreamed about during the nights on the rods. All frilly and satin. Miss Taylor insisted that Castor sleep in the same room with us. He began using it as a hangout. Even in the daytime.

Miss Taylor listened patiently enough when she came home from the studio. At the end of my speech, with my high voice trying to sound manly, I said, "Honey, it's either Castor or me."

I just barely won out.

I gave Castor to Lee Moore, even though Lee didn't seem to want him very much. Miss Taylor wouldn't speak to me for a month after that.

I bought her another dog.

A Pomeranian.

Miss Taylor had quite a few fans, but one of them annoyed the hell out of both of us. He was a Peeping Tom.

The bum would climb trees, wait in bushes and even try to get into our place for a look at her, particularly when she was dressing or asleep. He was a slippery guy but I didn't want to call the cops. It would have made me look pretty silly— the heavyweight champion of the world calling for help against some jerk degenerate.

So I rigged up some thin wires on our fences and grounds and attached them to a buzzer in our bedroom. I got me a shotgun, loaded it with rock salt, and stashed it under our bed. The Pomeranian didn't like it much. He was under there too by now.

One night Miss Taylor jabbed me awake and whispered, "The buzzer went off. He's here again."

Sleepily I reached under the bed for the shotgun. The damn Pomeranian bit me. I jerked my hand away and accidently pulled the trigger of the shotgun. The thing went off like a cannon and the rock-salt charge hit the Pomeranian right in the rump, sending him on his ear against the wall.

I had one hell of a time convincing Miss Taylor I hadn't done it on purpose. The Pomeranian refused to sleep in the same room with us after it came back from the vet's. I don't know what ever happened to the Peeping Tom.

CHAPTER 14

I TRIED IN OTHER WAYS TO KEEP MISS
Taylor Mrs. Dempsey. I even tried acting on the stage
with her, hoping this might hold our wobbly marriage together. I almost ruined the American theater, too.

I was getting a lot of "I can't get any good parts any
more because I'm married to a prize fighter," when one
day in Hollywood she got an offer to appear in a Broad-

way show to be produced by Sam Harris and directed by the great David Belasco.

She was happier than I had ever seen her before, and I could understand why. I had been around Hollywood long enough by this time to know that the best way a slipping star had of getting back into the chips was to appear in a legitimate theater and get good reviews.

There was one bad thing connected with the offer to Miss Taylor, though. Harris and Belasco were interested in signing her up only if I was the leading man.

"Honey," I apologized, "I know how much this means to you, but I can't act. You oughtta know that. You've seen me in those serials I made."

"David Belasco can make a good actor out of *anybody*," she said.

Miss Taylor was a very persuasive woman. So we signed. I was embarrassed by the contracts. They signed her for $300 a week, and me for $1,000.

The play was *The Big Fight*. I played the part of a fighter named Tiger. She was the beautiful dame I was in love with.

We got to New York the night before the first rehearsal, and the next day I met the great Belasco. I had never seen anything like it— wild wavy white hair, sometimes hanging down over his eyes, a collar like a priest's, a little guy who kept a limp wrist on his hips. Miss Taylor had given me a long lecture on who he was and what a figure he was in the theater, but my first thought on meeting the famous director was, Geez, the Great Director is also the Great "Character."

You could see that the cast was pretty impressed by me when we all gathered for our first reading from the script. I was bigger and stronger than everybody, of course. Then Belasco arrived, like an actor coming on stage, and opened the reading by making a little speech. It was a speech of welcome to me and encouragement to the other performers. He was thrilled, he was honored, this was a great play, it would run forever. Then he ordered the scripts distributed.

"You, Mr. Dempsey," he said, "are Tiger. Read me some of your lines. You are rough, you are tough, you are all man."

An actor showed me my place. I put my finger on it and stood up. I cleared my throat and started reading.

Everybody just stood there looking at me, astonished. Then they turned away, trying to keep from laughing. That damn voice of mine had gone almost soprano because I was nervous. The heavyweight champion of the world sounded more like a sissy than the Great Director did.

Then the big costar read. Miss Taylor holds a deep place in my memories. I loved her very much, and you never forget anybody you loved. On the other hand, she was almost as bad an actress as I was an actor and I wasn't any actor at all. If possible, her reading was as bad as mine.

Everybody was getting pretty nervous by now. The actors and actresses had that look of "Where can I get another job quick?" Mr. Belasco was walking up and down, and sometimes he'd run his hand through his mop of hair, especially when Miss Taylor and I were doing dialogue together.

He stopped me right in the middle of a word I was mispronouncing.

"Young man," he said, "can't you read?"

"Not very good, Mr. Belasco," I said. It was the only thing everybody seemed to agree with.

"Rehearsals are over," Mr. Belasco said sharply, and he started flouncing toward the wings. But he had something else to say. "Mr. Dempsey, go home and learn your ABC's." He let up on Miss Taylor, for he was a gentleman.

They decided to go on with the show anyway, so the rehearsals continued the next day. Miss Taylor and I had a big love scene in the script and that's what Mr. Belasco wanted to see acted out first thing off. I was embarrassed as hell making love right out in public, even with only actors and actresses watching.

"Go," said Mr. Belasco, like somebody starting a race at the Garden.

I took her in my arms and knocked her hat off.

"Stop," said Mr. Belasco. He minced over to me. "Mr. Dempsey," he said, real haughty like, "don't you know how to make love?"

Well, a lot of answers came to mind, but I was trying to please Miss Taylor.

"One makes love gently, Mr. Dempsey. Ever so gently."

I tried to make love to Miss Taylor gently. But that didn't please him either.

"Go home and rehearse," he said to me. "Cast dismissed."

It was very embarrassing.

We had a big fight scene in *The Big Fight* — the climax of the play, in fact. It was a crime what Mr. Belasco tried to do with it. He didn't know any more about fights than I knew about making love on a stage or reading lines right. Finally I couldn't stand it any more.

"Mr. Belasco, sir, you got this all wrong," I said, trying to help. "We'll all look crazy as hell if we do it your way. Now, in this scene where the fighters are being introduced, it's done this way— I'll show you."

He was looking at me, very cold, and my voice left me.

"Mr. Dempsey, would you like to direct this scene?"

"Well, I can show you the right way to do it."

Mr. Belasco could sneer so that it was like a punch. "Ladies and gentlemen," he said, turning to the rest of the cast like an after-dinner speaker. "Mr. Dempsey will now direct." He threw up his hands and stalked off to a seat in the farthest corner of the theater and just sulked there.

We all just stood there on the stage, like dummies. Miss Taylor was glaring at me like I had ruined her career. After a while Mr. Belasco came down the aisle and I said, "I didn't mean to hurt your feelings or tell you how to do your job. I thought you'd want to have it go the way it really goes." And I explained it to him and to the people who were going to be in the scene. He didn't speak until I had finished.

"Is that all, Mr. Dempsey?" he said.

"Yes, sir."

"Cast dismissed!" And off he pranced.

Sam Harris had guts enough to send us on the road.

Every night was awful, like I expected, but one night in New Haven sticks out in my mind after all these years.

The fellow I fought in the big fight scene was Ralph Smith, a heavyweight who had done a little acting around Hollywood between club fights. Ralph was a freak. He stood almost seven feet tall and weighed 280. The script called for him to take a dive in the first round. Every night as he hit the deck I marveled at the way he did it. He was a real artist at being knocked down. Sometimes I wondered whether he had learned this on the stage or in the ring. Wherever he learned it, old Ralph could really dive. Every time he went down for the count, shaking the stage and the scenery, the audience thought I had knocked him out for real.

Well, that night in New Haven the show had been laying its usual egg right up to the fight scene. That woke up some of the people. Ralph and I were introduced and, on cue, I went out after him as usual. We mixed like we always had for a minute or two, then I threw the usual right and stepped back to watch another great performance—Ralph going into the tank.

He hit me a right on the chin that made me cockeyed. Somebody had sense enough to ring the bell.

The fellow who wrote the show hadn't written in anything about a second round. But we had one. I figured Ralph was, you know, trying to build up his part or something. We went out there and he kept swinging away at me real good.

When he came out for the fourth round I went into a clinch and whispered to him, "Hey, you bum, go down.

You're ruining the show." He fought his way out of the clinch, but I got him in close again and said, "Listen, if you don't go down and let the show go on I'm gonna flatten you for real." He took a punch at me that might have killed a horse. Everybody was awake now.

In the fifth round I had to do it. I hooked him in the belly and when he doubled over I hit him on the side of the head with a right and down he went, just like he used to when he was acting. But this wasn't acting.

After the show I was boiling. I went into the room where he was dressing and said, "What the hell were you trying to do out there— fight?" I guess it was a silly question, for that's what the script said he was supposed to do.

Ralph rubbed his jaw. "I'm sorry, Jack," he said. "You hit me so hard in that first round I didn't know where I was from then on."

I knew just how he felt. I didn't know where I was at out there either.

The Big Fight actually got to Broadway. Ripley should have had that in his cartoon.

While I was dressing for opening night Sam Harris came to my room. He said, "Jack, listen to me carefully. This is very important. It must be done right. It will mean a lot to Mr. Belasco." I liked Sam, so I listened, even though he could have thought of a better argument than that last sentence.

"Now, when the show's over tonight you'll take your bows, but after you do there will be a lot of yells for Mr. Belasco." I could see that that was all arranged, the yells for Mr. Belasco.

"Fine," I said. "But what's that got to do with me?"

Sam had been through all this before, I guess. He said, "Mr. Belasco won't be there when they yell for him. He won't come out to take a bow."

"He goes home early?" I asked him.

"No," said Sam, with a kind of sigh. "He'll be hiding."

I didn't understand. "How the hell can I bring him on if I can't find him?"

"You'll find him, don't worry about that," Sam said. "He'll tell you where he'll be hiding."

"*Who'll* tell me where he'll be hiding?"

Sam was a patient man and a great guy. "Mr. Belasco will tell you in advance where he'll be hiding," he explained. "Then, when you find him, he'll struggle. He won't want to come on stage."

I could understand that, having seen the show and acted in it.

"You'll sort of drag him on, like it's against his will. But once he's on he'll make a little speech."

I scratched my head. "Sam, if Mr. Belasco don't want to take a bow and make a speech all he has to do is say so," I said. It didn't make sense to me.

"Jack," he said, "Mr. Belasco is a genius. Geniuses are peculiar. He wants very much to take a bow and make a speech. But he doesn't want people to think he wants to take a bow and make a speech."

"He's a phony old bastard, Sam," I said. "But what the hell, I'll do what you want."

When the final curtain fell on opening night the applause was less than I used to get winning some of those saloon fights years before. But, sure enough, the yells for Mr. Belasco started. He was very popular with ushers.

I came to front and center in the bright lights and told the audience that our great director was hiding somewhere, but that I'd go backstage and try to find him and talk him into coming out and taking a bow.

He wasn't hard to find. He was three feet inside the wings and all made up with that pancake stuff and eyebrow pencil. But for some crazy reason I didn't understand he gave me a battle about coming out to do the thing he wanted to. He started to drag his heels and beat at me with his little fists. I gave him a yank, or maybe I tripped him, I don't remember. Anyway, he fell on the seat of his pants.

It made Mr. Belasco pretty angry. He sat there on the floor with his hair over his eyes and they were glaring at me. I reached down and grabbed him by the ankles and pulled him out on stage. If Sam Harris wanted him on stage I was going to get him there.

It was a hell of an entrance, even for Mr. Belasco. I guess I pulled him too fast, because he lost his sitting position and was flat on his back with his head bumping and his arms waving when I got him as far as center front. The people out front were in hysterics.

When I let go of Mr. Belasco's ankles he got up, brushed himself and went right into his act.

"Ladies and gentlemen, this is the greatest moment of my life," he said. "I've produced and directed many great plays and players. But this great, great play you saw tonight is the crowning achievement of my long theatrical career."

The guy actually sounded like he meant it. And then he started to cry. The audience applauded. The more he cried the more they applauded. Then he turned off the tears, held up his hands for silence and continued.

"Imagine the honor of directing these great performers!" he said, like we were all named Barrymore or something. "And working with Jack Dempsey, this great man, this fine actor, this magnificent champion of champions." All I wanted to hear him say was something about Miss Taylor, and he did in the next sentence. "And his beautiful, talented wife, the great Hollywood star Estelle Taylor."

It was the best job of acting in that theater all night. Better even than Ralph Smith's dive. But the Great Director wasn't finished. His act hadn't reached its finale.

He fainted. Right into my arms.

Sam hadn't told me about this one, but Mr. Belasco did. His eyes were rolled back like a man in a fit. He rolled his head as I held him. Then he whispered, "Carry me off."

And so I did.

As soon as we were off stage Mr. Belasco hopped out of my arms like a canary. We didn't see much of him during the rest of the six terrible weeks *The Big Fight* lasted. Mr. Belasco knew a turkey when he saw one. His interest in the show had ended with his opening-night performance.

The Big Fight wasn't the first, or even the worst, of my

life in show business. My life in that business started out
with getting the hook, as I described. It ended getting
hooked. In between, I made good money with maybe less
talent than any stage character ever had. Kearns and I
had a vaudeville act that would take us from coast to coast
at $7,500 a week almost any time we wanted. We should've
been arrested for stealing money. Yet we played two
stands at the Palace in New York when it was the last
word in vaudeville, and we set a record at Loew's State
which I believe is still on the books.

Kearns was a real hambone. He loved to be on stage.
But as much as he loved it he never got around to learning
any lines. I never got around to remembering the ones I
learned. So we'd come out on stage carrying newspapers,
open them up and go into one of those "I see by the papers" routines. Our jokes were pasted in the paper. Even
then we might read the wrong punch line and foul
things up.

Then I'd shadowbox, hit the bag and jump rope. Lots
of fighters can do those things good enough for the price
of admission. But I was always a bum in a gym. I liked to
train, sure, but I was awkward and clumsy when I tried to
hit something filled with sand or air instead of meat.

The amazing thing is that we almost always got good
reviews. The vaudeville critics were never tough like the
legit critics. Also, Kearns could always find an angle for
the sports writers who called on us when we went into a
new town. We got an awful lot of publicity and it helped
fill theaters wherever we went.

I toured burlesque, offering $1,000 to any local yokel

who stayed three rounds with me. None of them ever did. I don't say that in any bragging way. In the first place almost any pro can lick the toughest guy in town. In the second place the first of the three rounds, if I needed three, lasted five minutes— two minutes more than legal. The second round, if the fellow was still in there winging at me, lasted maybe ten minutes. A third round, if necessary, could last all night. You can't have too much respect for a sucker, and any amateur who climbs into a ring to fight the heavyweight champion of the world is a sucker. Furthermore, I figured anybody who lasted three of those rounds with me wasn't a real home town boy. He was a pro trying to make a sucker out of me or trying to get himself a rep by flattening me.

For a spell there I traveled with the Sells-Floto Circus at $2,500 a week, taking on all comers, but I remember the horse I rode in the parade better than I remember the poor guys I flattened.

As for the movies, there was a serial named *Daredevil Jack*, with Josie Sedgwick, which I don't think ever ended. Woody Van Dyke was the director. Then another serial called *Fight and Win,* and a full-length job with Miss Taylor named *Manhattan Madness.*

These films didn't take very long to shoot, of course, and as a matter of fact they were shot in an unusual way. Or, at least, they were after I had been in Hollywood for a time. In the beginning of my movie career we'd schedule the fight scene whenever it was convenient. But eventually it was always the last sequence shot. That was because the actor I fought usually quit the movie.

I remember slapping and giving smelling salts to a good-looking young fellow I had accidentally knocked out in the fight sequence of a film (there was always a fight sequence) and hearing him say when he came to, "Dammit, Mr. Dempsey, I'm an actor, not a prize fighter— and you're a prize fighter, not an actor."

I was ashamed of myself, but I just couldn't learn to pull a punch. There wasn't any killer instinct connected with it. I didn't want to hurt those fellows. It was just that I was a lousy actor. That made me nervous before the cameras, being a lousy actor. And oddly enough I was most nervous in the ring sequences. I could never satisfy a director with my pulled punches. I'd have to do it over and over, and finally in desperation I'd cut the line too thin between a fake and the real McCoy and down would go some nice guy who shouldn't have been in there fighting his mother, much less me.

The actors would raise hell when this happened. But the directors always liked it.

It's a funny thing, but years and years later, when I had been around long enough to have picked up some stage presence, I started getting paid just what my original talent deserved. Nothing. Not long after the big war I was signed as star of a traveling show put on by a Southern patent-medicine outfit. The people turned out like armies, but for some mysterious reason the show ran out of money. Suddenly the guys who hired me couldn't be found. I was out $17,000 due me.

But as I looked back over the years when I was paid well for reading badly, remembering worse, and knocking over poor bums Miss Taylor could have beaten, I had a feeling that things were just evening out.

I'll finish with Miss Taylor, for she was the cause of most of my life in show business. She got the idea after a while that I was running around, which I wasn't. She got it mostly from a story out of New York. Seems that I was in the big town staying at a Fifth Avenue hotel when my old pal Joe Benjamin dropped by. Joe was suffering from the shorts. I had turned my business affairs over to a friend of mine named Gene Normile at the time, so I sent Joe to Gene. Gene wouldn't let him have any money.

So Joe came back to me and said, "You're worse than Normile. You kept him from giving me that money, you cheap bastard."

I don't like being called cheap. An argument started. Joe took a punch at me, so I slapped him. I didn't punch my old pal. Just a slap. But it knocked him back against a hotel door and the whole panel of the door gave way. Joe landed in some guy's room.

Well, there was hell to pay. The guy called for the manager, the manager called for the cops, and the cops called for the reporters and photographers. The next day the tabloids carried a picture of Joe with a black eye and a story that claimed Joe and I had had a fight over one of the most beautiful show girls in New York, Hazel Forbes.

The story hit the Los Angeles papers. Miss Taylor wasn't pleased one little bit.

With that, and the feeling she had that I was holding back her career, the end was soon coming. One morning without raising her voice she said to me, "Get out of here."

"Do you really mean that?" I asked her. It was hard to believe.

"Yes, I do."

So I went to Reno after making a property settlement.

It was an expensive parting. I bought back a house I had given her for $200,000, and I added another $100,000 to soothe her aches and pains.

Miss Taylor was a nice woman, really. Whatever she cost me, she was worth it. I'm sorry it didn't work out better.

But that's getting a little ahead of the story.

CHAPTER 15

FOR TWO OR THREE OF THE YEARS BE-
tween the 1923 fight against Firpo and the night in 1926
when Gene Tunney took my title from me, the biggest
challenger in the world was Harry Wills. At least he was
No. 1 challenger in the newspapers and among the politicians.

» 179 «

Even to this day I occasionally hear or read that I ducked him and therefore must have figured at the time he would have licked me.

Wills was made for me. I could always lick those big slow guys. I personally never ducked him. I thought the fight should take place. Why the hell shouldn't I have fought him? I was champion of the world.

For a time there I thought we had a match. I was on the rocks with Kearns at the time and trying to do my own business. Floyd Fitzsimmons announced he was going to put the fight on in Chicago. He invited Wills and me to South Bend, Indiana, for the signing. There was a lot of publicity. Wills signed first and got a $50,000 down payment on whatever his share was to be. Maybe that was all of it. Anyway, he got it.

I was supposed to get a million dollars. How about that? The first payment of the million was to be $300,000, the minute I signed. The rest was to come between then and fight time.

I signed all right, but instead of giving me the $300,000 check Floyd gave me his hand and said that he'd have the money the next day.

The next day he tried to give me a check for $25,000.

"Look, Floyd, I'm your friend," I said. "I'm trying to make you some money. You gave Wills fifty. I'm not taking twenty-five. There's something screwy."

"Jack, all I've got is this check for twenty-five," he said, "but there's more where this came from. Don't you worry."

He looked like *he* needed it.

"I tell you what," I said. "I'll take you to a bank I know and introduce you. You get that twenty-five in cash and put it in your pocket. When your people come up with the other two-seventy-five I'll give you this contract I've signed. In the meantime, you just keep the twenty-five."

I got a big reception at the bank. I introduced Floyd to the president and started to explain about the check.

"Boy," the president said to one of his assistants, "take this down and get the money right away."

"You'd better call the bank it's drawn on," I suggested. He wouldn't listen to me for a while and kept talking fights. Finally I insisted. So he put through a call.

He got his call through just as his assistant came into the office with $25,000 in cash. The man at the other bank told him there wasn't a penny in the account the check was drawn on. He was very grateful.

I raised hell with Fitzsimmons and blew town. His partners sued me for a couple of years after that for things like breach of contract.

Another reason I never fought Wills was because he was a Negro. Not that the color of a fellow meant anything to me. I fought Negroes. Knocked some of them out with a punch. Had a real hard time with John Lester Johnson. In Wills's case, others made the decision.

Tex Rickard didn't want the match. Today it's hard to understand the kind of reasoning of those days. For example, when Jack Johnson won the title he had to go all the way to New South Wales to beat Tommy Burns, because Burns was a white man. That was 1908. Until then the heavyweight championship never bothered too many people one way or another. But when a Negro got the title, well, that was something like the Johnstown flood.

I've written about how I changed a face on my punching bag as a kid. But later on, when I had some sense and knew more, I found out just what it meant to a lot of people to have Johnson as champion. It was all right to have colored champions in the lighter divisions, like Joe Gans or somebody like that. But many people, accustomed to Sullivan, Corbett, Fitzsimmons and Jeffries, considered it an insult to the white race that Johnson should hold the heavyweight title— and Johnson didn't do much to make them think any other way. Every white fighter who won two in a row, or even looked like he could fight, was called a "white hope."

One of the reasons Tex was against matching me with Wills was the criticism he had gotten years before for putting on the Johnson–Jeffries fight. He had been accused of humiliating the white race and things like that.

William Muldoon, a tough old geezer who ran the New York State Athletic Commission, was against the Wills fight for another reason: he thought it might end up in a race riot, no matter who won.

Rickard spoke mysteriously about "Washington" not wanting the fight. In New York, others demanded that it be held, and some of them could have been thinking of the Harlem vote in the next election. Fights had that much importance in those days.

Anyway, the men whose words or experience I trusted at that time said I couldn't fight Wills, and I never did.

Kearns and Rickard had made a big fellow out of me, where before I had been a hobo. Muldoon was a man I had a lot of respect for. He had trained John L. Sullivan with the help of a baseball bat, and he was the kind of guy who would reach up and snatch a cigar out of your mouth and grind it under his foot if he caught you smoking in his house or even in his presence. None of them had any doubt that I could beat Wills. Nor did I. But I'm sorry now the fight never came off.

Wills was mostly a victim of bigotry. He was gypped out of his crack at the title because people with a lot of money tied up in the boxing game thought that a fight against me, if it went wrong, might kill the business. People of importance still worried about "white supremacy," race riots, the Negro vote— which might swing somewhere else if I flattened Wills— and things like that.

Harry's dead now. He died without ever knowing how he would have come out. But he lived to see a day when the Negro fighter really came into his own in the heavyweight division and changed boxing history.

Only ten years after all these troubles I've mentioned, a man named John Roxborough, a college fellow, called up Jimmy Johnston, the boxing promoter at Madison Square Garden, and asked him to match up a young Negro heavyweight named Joe Louis.

Johnston offered Roxborough peanuts, though Louis was beginning to pile up what became one of the great records of all time. Roxborough gave Jimmy an argument, but Jimmy cut him off and said, "Listen, you know a Negro fighter can't get anywhere unless we help him, don't you?"

Roxborough waited a little bit and said, "I'm a Negro, too, Mr. Johnston." Then he hung up. That's when Mike Jacobs, who had handled the ticket sales for Rickard and bankrolled some of his fights, got into the promotion business. Mike put on a few fights the Garden wouldn't handle, and in time he came closer to being a second Tex Rickard than anyone else in the boxing game, thanks to Louis and a lot of help he had from sports writers like Runyon, Bill Farnsworth and Eddie Frayne.

You might wonder now why I wouldn't say to Kearns and Rickard, "To hell with you, I'm going to fight this guy Wills."

Kearns and I were beginning to split up and Rickard and I were getting closer all the time. If either had asked me to stand on my head and fight somebody, I would have thought seriously about doing it. Each had a tremendous influence on me. Kearns's was sloughing off but was still important. Rickard's was going into high gear.

Let me tell you about those two. I'll start with Kearns.

Jack Kearns was born in upstate Michigan and nobody remembers just when. His name was Leo McKiernan. He may have changed it when he started fighting.

After my mother and my brother Bernie, Doc was the most important figure in my life. I'll always be grateful to him. I think it's possible to be grateful to a guy without liking him. I doubt if I would have become heavyweight champion if it hadn't been for Kearns. He was a great manager, a great judge of fighters.

Training camps bored Doc. He didn't spend as much time around them as he should have. But when he was around he was invaluable in the business of preparing me for a fight. His most important contribution was his knowledge of boxing styles. He could spot a weakness or a strength in an opponent before anybody else could. He was the greatest expert I ever met. He was never wrong.

Doc hired the best sparring partners available. He hired guys he knew could fight in the style of the fellow I was training to meet.

He was a fantastic press agent. He had more guts, or gall, talking to newspapermen than anybody I ever saw. I can still hear him saying to guys with pencils and paper in their hands, "My man will knock that bum out with one punch," when I wasn't sure of any such thing. But many times, to my surprise, I made him look good as a picker of fights.

Kearns got along swell with sports writers. He was a great party thrower, which they enjoyed. They got as much of a kick out of his gift of gab as they did out of his booze. Nobody ever went to Kearns and came away without a new angle on an old story.

One thing I personally didn't like about him was that I used to get the feeling he thought I was a Grade A boob. Once, during one of our vaudeville turns, he got mixed up and introduced me as John L. Sullivan. Before a fight he used to give me long pep talks I didn't need, and when he wasn't telling me how great I was he was telling me how great *he* was.

I guess we started to drift apart when I realized, looking around New York, that he dressed and acted like somebody off Salt Lake City's Commercial Street and that I was trying to act just like him. We began going with different groups to the same places, places like Texas Guinan's or the Silver Slipper. He could tell me how to fight Carpentier or Firpo but he couldn't or wouldn't tell me how to use a fork, and I wanted to know that too.

The only bad bargain I ever knew him make as my manager was settling for the guarantee instead of the percentage in the Carpentier fight— the deal that cost us $150,000.

Our arrangement was never on paper. In fact, I never could get Kearns to put anything on paper. And there was the rub. When he matched me against Willie Meehan the first time, our oral agreement was that he would get one third of my purse after expenses had been deducted. In no time it was an even split.

Now, a fifty-fifty split between any performer and his agent is ridiculous and in many states it's illegal. But Kearns got this division from me because he was worth it. He delivered. I did not, nor do I now, begrudge him a penny of the maybe two million dollars or so he earned out of me.

Doc got half of everything— movies, vaudeville, circuses, whatever appeared in print under my name and I was paid for, even real-estate investments. It was always kind of a loose transaction. He knew everything; I was too dumb for him to explain things to.

"Here's your end, kid," he used to say to me after I had been through a fight.

When we first hooked up I was grateful. My end was becoming as much as $500 . . . $800. This was gold-mine stuff. It never even occurred to me to ask what the gross or net of the fight had been. But as the fights got bigger, and my reputation started growing, the newspapers began printing the gross and the net of my fights, and sometimes even the share that I had earned. I'd take out a pencil and divide that sum in half, but what Kearns had given me was never as much as I thought I had coming.

"How come?" I finally asked him.

"Expenses, kid, expenses," he said. I nodded. It seemed important. Then he'd disappear for a couple of weeks.

But then came the time when each fight was beginning to mean a fortune, and in a day when a fellow thought as little about income taxes as you do now about, let's say, the cigarette tax.

As time went on and I got a little more sense I began to demand an accounting. In a way, Kearns changed too. He stopped laughing at me. He'd say, "You're right, kid. I'll get an accounting together right away." Then he'd blow, and I wouldn't be able to find him for days or even weeks.

Kearns handled at least five million dollars I earned and never gave me an accounting in writing.

Why did I stand for it so many years? That's very easy to explain. When the money started rolling in I still had calluses on my can from the rods, and every buck seemed like found money. When I'd earn some vaudeville money, which always seemed like stealing to me, and Kearns would say, "I'm short this week, kid, so let me hold it all this time," it was all right by me.

It mounted up until he was in to me for $150,000 by the time of the Firpo fight. I got that back by getting up earlier than he did the day after the fight.

For example, I had the shorts when I got back to Hollywood with Miss Taylor after our European honeymoon. I thought I had money coming to me from Universal and I drove around— in the Rolls Royce, no less— to collect it.

There wasn't a quarter there. "Your manager picked it up for you," the cashier said.

Half of it was his, although he hadn't lifted a finger or even watched the movie. This money I didn't want. But I did want my half. I went looking for him, steaming, but when I finally found him he handled me like a real chump. I never did find out whether he had really collected any money or not.

We got down to hard words over the house I had bought for my mother— the big house I had thought would be everything she wanted in life. Kearns traded it, without even telling me, in on a Los Angeles hotel.

That house meant something to me. It meant something to me, too, that he hadn't even bothered to tell me what he was doing.

I gave him hell. I said, "You're through. I don't want to see you again, have anything to do with you again. If you want to stick around as my fight manager it will be on a straight one-third cut, but that's all. We're finished in every other way."

"I'll be what I've always been with you, or nothing," Doc said.

"Good," I said. "You're now nothing." We split up our real-estate holdings.

That was the end but not the finish. Kearns said, "You'll

never fight again." And when I did, he started a series of suits that lasted for years.

One of the first things Kearns brought up in those years of suits was a contract I was supposed to have signed with him in New York, acknowledging him as my legal manager and entitling him to 33⅓ per cent (the legal limit) of my purses. I had never signed the thing, actually. It was a piece of paper we needed before the commission sanctioned the Firpo fight. I paid Kearns 50 per cent, not 33⅓, after that fight— as usual— minus what he owed me but plus a bill for "expenses."

Now he dug up that old contract, and in court it looked like his case ace. But you never know about courts.

"How much money did you get from Mr. Dempsey for the Firpo fight?" the judge asked Doc.

It seemed like a reasonable question, but Doc wouldn't answer.

The judge then asked Kearns, "Did you file a tax return on your income from Mr. Dempsey?"

Kearns again refused to answer.

The judge leaned over and said, "Mr. Kearns, you answer that question or get off the stand."

Doc stepped down, and his case was over.

You could write a book about Kearns, but in the end it might come down to this: He mistook gratitude for stupidity.

CHAPTER **16**

"I WANT YOU TO FIGHT GENE TUNNEY,
right here in New York," Rickard said to me, when it was
decided the Wills fight couldn't be held.

Tunney?

"Fine," I said. I started remembering what I knew about
him: Just a boxer. That was all I could think of.

My end of the net was of more interest. Tex was going

to give me 50 per cent. I had picked up Gene Normile as my manager. Gene was a nice guy who worked for my friend Baron Long, who ran Tia Juana. He had been a telegrapher and reporter on Coast papers and knew his way around. Gene took care of a lot of the little things. Actually, I had become my own manager. The years with Kearns, the years of never having much to say about myself, now made me want to handle everything myself. It wasn't very smart, but I guess it was natural.

The New York State Athletic Commission wouldn't sanction the Tunney fight in New York. It said I'd fight Wills or nobody, and that turned out to be a break for everybody. Rickard switched the fight to Philadelphia and it drew twice what it would have done in New York.

It was Sesquicentennial Year in Philadelphia, and the people fought to buy seats right down to the rainy night of the fight itself. Tex scaled the ringside at $50 a seat and it reached back to the suburbs in that big stadium. Nobody will ever know how much was charged by and made by the scalpers. Or by the more or less legitimate ticket men like Mike Jacobs.

Years later Mike told of being approached on the day of the fight by Boo Boo Hoff, the Philadelphia mob fellow, who said he had to have twenty-five more ringside seats to take care of his friends in Philadelphia and Pennsylvania politics. Mike said the whole ringside was sold out.

Boo Boo shook his head. "I've *got* to get them," he said. He pulled out a roll that would choke an elephant and counted off twenty-five $1,000 bills and handed them to Mike.

» 191 «

Mike made some quick changes in the ringside, moving in chairs, moving people who wouldn't gripe too much, handed over the twenty-five tickets and pocketed the $25,000. Boo Boo put the tickets in his pocket and started away.

"Just a minute," Mike said in his crabby way. "You forgot to pay me for the *tickets.* They're fifty bucks each." And Boo Boo paid.

You couldn't hold a big fight in those days without doing some kind of business with the mob in charge of the town.

The mob fixed that fight. It was a crazy kind of fix, because neither fighter knew anything about it. A few days before the fight one of Hoff's gorillas came to Billy Gibson, Tunney's manager, and asked him how Tunney felt about the fight.

"My boy has trained hard and thinks he can win," Billy said.

The guy looked at Gibson, sizing him up, I guess, and said, "Would you like to be sure?"

Bill said anybody would like to be sure.

Out of that talk came a plan, or a fix, based on what you might call a calculated risk. It was a cinch, they figured, that sometime during the fight I'd hit Tunney low. The law of averages would see to that, for I always threw a lot of leather and from all positions, and ever since I was a kid I had been climbing into rings with just one thought in mind: Kill the guy before he can kill you.

If I hit him low and he showed signs of being in distress, or if he went down, the fight was to be stopped long enough for Tunney to be examined. Then an official would announce that I had fouled Tunney and Gene was the new heavyweight champion of the world. The story was that the mob had reached the officials.

Tunney didn't need any help from outside to beat me that night.

It's been written a thousand times that I was doped before the first Tunney fight. Something like that wouldn't have been hard to do. I did feel a little groggy in the hours leading up to the fight. But there's a better chance that it was a combination of other things.

I had three law suits pending. Kearns was after me with writs, court orders and attempts to hold up my money and even the fight; I was afraid to shake hands with anybody, for process servers usually used a handshake to serve a "plaster" on me. Normile was a nice guy, and the guys around me knew the boxing business, but I felt I had to run my own training camps— first in California, then at Luther's place in Saratoga. I couldn't concentrate on training. I hadn't picked up much weight— I was just under 190— but I couldn't untrack myself. I had been out of the ring for three years.

Tunney was just a boxer, I kept telling myself. That was about the only comforting thing I could think of in those busy days leading up to the fight. I'd move in through those light punches and flatten him as soon as I caught him. Who the hell was Tunney? Sure, I knew all about how he prepared for this chance over the years, how he took special exercises to increase the size of his neck and make him able to take a punch better, how he used to carry sponge balls in each hand night and day, working and gripping them, to make his hands bigger and stronger.

And I knew he was a Marine. So did the crowd. There were boos for me.

There's never been a crowd like it, before or since. By the time the last rain-soaked guy got in, the total attendance was 120,757. The gate was, up to then, September 23, 1926, the biggest of all time— $1,895,733, out of which my end came to about $800,000. The gamblers had a long memory. They made me the favorite, two and a half to one.

Tunney walked right out of his corner and hit me in the mouth with a good straight right. A couple of inches lower and it would have knocked me down.

I never caught up.

I was slower than I thought, or Gene was faster. I found myself blaming the wet ring, but it didn't seem to bother Gene's footwork. When I'd finally get what I knew was a good footing, he'd be gone. He glided around the ring like he was on ice. He jumped a lot and backed up, and wherever I went, looking for him, he stuck that left of his into my face, keeping me off balance, piling up points. And now and then he'd stop me with a stiff right. I was wide open, looking for a big one.

Gene won it easy.

It's a sad thing to hear the fellow with the microphone yell into it, "The winner and *new* heavyweight champion of the world . . ." when you're the old one.

I walked across the ring to Gene's corner, put my arm around him and said, "Gene, you're a great champion. Lots of luck to you."

I started back for my own corner, and to leave the ring.

And then something happened that had never happened to me before.

The people were cheering for me, clapping for me, calling out my name in a way I had never heard before. I never realized how much I had hungered for a sound like that, and now here it was— on the night I blew my title.

Losing was the making of me.

Miss Taylor came down late from New York. She didn't want to see the fight, and I didn't want her to see it. You shouldn't let your wife see you fight.

She was in the living room of the hotel suite when I came in with my handlers. The rest of the mob had gone to Tunney's hotel.

Miss Taylor had heard the bad news, of course. She looked at my beat-up face.

"What happened, Ginsberg?" she asked.

"Honey," I said, "I forgot to duck."

Everybody figured there would be an automatic announcement about a rematch. It all added up. My alibi was that I had been out of action for three years, had a lot of aggravations, couldn't train right, and things like that. Nowadays there wouldn't be any question about a rematch.

But Rickard was a peculiar man. He never believed in a rematch unless the loser not only had a good alibi but proved to the fans that he could fight as good as or better than he had fought the last time.

"I'm going to match you against Jack Sharkey, the winner to fight Tunney," Rickard said.

He was the boss. In a way, he had become my boss, too.

He was like a father to me. For instance, he saw that Gene Normile couldn't handle my affairs, so he lined up Leo P. Flynn as my manager.

Flynn gave me some good advice the first day we were together.

"Sharkey's a better fighter than Tunney," he said. "Get that in your head. And remember this: He's got one weakness. He can't take it around the body. When you get in there you keep punching to the body until he drops his hands. When he drops them, let that right hand go and then the left and knock him out."

It's just as well I had Flynn around before the Sharkey fight, and Rickard to lean on.

Enough went wrong. I was still being sued for not fighting Wills two or three years before. Kearns had all kinds of papers out on me. I wasn't looking any better in the gym, and that was saying something.

But the big thing was Johnny. My brother.

Johnny wanted to be a fighter. He was a year older than I, one of the handsomest guys you ever saw, wonderful personality, smile and all that. He could box as good as anybody, but the second he was tagged the fight was over.

So after I set things up for my mother and later Miss Taylor around the movie business, Johnny came to Hollywood to try acting. Everybody liked him, and he liked everybody. He began making the party rounds of the town right away. You could hear "This is Johnny Dempsey— you know, the champ's brother," all over the place. It was pretty exciting, after Utah.

I don't know who introduced Johnny to dope. I wish to

God I did know. I do know that one of his pals was Wally Reid, who died an addict.

Nothing helped. I had him in and out of a dozen hospitals and clinics, treated by every good doctor and psychiatry fellow I could hire. Good old Bernie, Johnny's idol, talked to him for hours, days, weeks and couldn't get through to him. Neither could Joe. My mother talked and cried, and it was all wasted.

My money was there and it was used. But my money, in the long run, only made him hate me. I finally wouldn't let him have any dough when I knew he was going to spend it on the junk. He wanted to kill me for that.

Johnny had married a wonderful woman. She and my mother were the two finest women I ever knew. She left Johnny in 1927, not long before the Sharkey fight in July. Any other woman would have quit him years before. She went back to her home in Utica, New York, and Johnny followed her. I guess he must have pleaded with her to come back to him, and I guess she refused.

Anyway, he shot her dead and killed himself.

It was seventy-two hours before the Sharkey fight.

Sharkey gave me living hell for the first five rounds. During that stretch he was as good a fighter as I've ever seen. He moved like a good middleweight, stuck, hooked, hit, everything. I thought he was going to knock me out. He couldn't miss me with his left.

Once more I could feel the crowd was with me. In the sixth, after Flynn had yelled it into my ear in the corner enough times, I started going for Sharkey's middle. I gave it to him pretty good, and I could see right off he didn't like it. In the middle of the seventh, after I had hit him half a dozen times around the belt, he stepped back, dropped his hands, turned his head to Jock O'Sullivan, the ref, and yelled, "Hey, he's hittin' me low!"

I hit him with one of the last good punches of my life. It was everything I could throw. I couldn't miss. His chin was sticking out there, unprotected. Sharkey went down and it was all over.

What was I going to do— write him a letter?

The crowd went crazy. I remember an old telegrapher in the first press row jumping up and pounding on the ring apron with his fist. He had only two or three teeth in his head, and he kept yelling, "That'll show these bastards they can't lick us old guys, Jack."

I didn't feel old any more.

It was a real good touch: a crowd of 75,000 and a gross gate of $1,083,530, my fourth million-dollar gate. I made half a million.

But it was to be followed two months later by the gate which, I guess, will stand as a record for all time. I mean the gate of the second Tunney fight. It drew 104,943 fans into Soldier Field, Chicago, and a gate of $2,658,660.

They don't make them like that any more.

Rickard thought the Sharkey fight was enough for 1927. He wanted to hold the second Tunney fight over to 1928 and give it a year's build-up. But he was talked out of it by the man whose friendship he needed in Chicago, the millionaire boxing commissioner and big-game hunter, George

Goetz. Goetz had planned a long trip to Africa in 1928 and would have missed the fight if it had been held then.

So Tex finally nodded okay, and I went back into training almost before they had cleaned up the joint after the Sharkey fight.

I beefed a little. The next year would have suited me better too. I still had those legal headaches. Kearns wouldn't let me sleep. Miss Taylor was sick a lot of the time. Our marriage was really rocky.

Tex tried to cheer me up.

"That Tunney," he said, hitting me on the back. "*I* can lick him."

I couldn't.

So much has been written about that one over the years that sometimes I get a little mixed up myself.

I won't forget the seventh, though. You don't forget any second of something you waited seventeen rounds for— ten through the first fight and now seven in the second fight. It was my first good shot at Gene. What I remember is that I got to him with a pretty good right, and then I hit him with a real good left hook.

He started to go. I hit him seven times while he was going down, hit him with all the punches I had been trying to hit him with in the ring and in my sleep for the past year.

I thought he was finished. I thought I had become the first guy ever to win back the heavyweight title after blowing it.

I forgot all about a rule they had put in not long before that. It said that a man scoring a knockdown should "immediately retire to a neutral corner."

What the hell is a neutral corner? When you're fighting—or at least when you're fighting the way I used to fight—all of the corners look alike, and it's hard to stop what you're doing, standing over a guy and waiting for him to get up, and start figuring out which corner is farthest away from where it's all happening.

The new rule said something else. It said that if there was a knockdown the referee was supposed to take the guy who threw the punch to a neutral corner, then come back and pick up the count in unison with the count of the knockdown timekeeper.

Well, I didn't go to a neutral corner. I forgot all about the rules. But I was finally pushed to one. Gene was still on the canvas, where I had knocked him.

After the ref pushed me into the neutral corner he came back to where Gene was and started counting. But instead of picking up the count of the knockdown timekeeper and saying, let's say, "Nine . . . ten . . . out," he started from one. Gene got up at seven or eight.

I'll never really know whether he could or could not have gotten up during what should have been the first section of the count. Gene has often told me he could have, and I have no reason not to believe him. Gene's a great guy.

He took the count, whatever it was, and that's what any smart fighter would have done. In boxing, take what they give you.

Then he got up. There have been millions of words written about how he went on the bicycle after that. That's a lot of hooey. Sure, he backed up until he got his bearings. Then he continued to beat me. He had been winning on points up to then almost as easy as in the first fight. I chased him and couldn't keep up. Tired, I set my feet and beckoned to him to come in and fight. That seems pretty silly when I look back on it, though a lot of guys wrote some nice things about that. Why should he do what I wanted him to do?

If I have any resentment about that fight, and I don't really have much, it was over something that people have forgotten.

Tunney knocked *me* down in the ninth. People forget that. The ref pushed him in the direction of a neutral corner, jumped back to me, and this time he picked up the count of the knockdown timekeeper.

That completed the reason why so many people, for so many years after that and even to this day, figured I was robbed.

I don't think I was. Everything happens for the best. In the years since then I've lost track of the number of times reporters and just plain people have asked me about that fight. I never talk about the long count. Gene says he could have gotten up at any time. The official said it *wasn't* a long count. You go by what the official says. Maybe Gene could have gotten up. Maybe not. Everything happens for the best.

There were a lot of stories that we were going to be rematched, and this time there might have been more reason for it than after the first fight. There were stories that I turned it down because I was afraid Gene might blind me with his jabs. There were stories that Gene wanted no part of me because the seventh-round knockdown had shown him I could flatten him if I fought him again.

Actually, what happened in my case was that Miss Taylor wanted me to quit and I figured I had enough money. Besides, I knew that every new fight meant more lawsuits and aggravations.

Gene was anxious to get out too. His friends were millionaire sportsmen like Bernard Gimbel, and bankers, big businessmen, professors and so forth. His ambition was to retire undefeated, with one more fight to serve as a kind of farewell, and then be a part of that group the rest of his life. (It was to work out that way, too, the farewell match being his fight with Tom Heeney in June 1928.)

Lord knows we had the cash reserve to hang up our gloves. My "short end" of the net after the Chicago fight was $425,000— the biggest amount a nonchampion ever got for fighting. Gene's end, of course, remains the all-time record, and I can't see how it will ever be topped.

He gave Tex Rickard his personal check for $9,554.46, and Tex handed him a check for $1,000,000. Gene's actual purse had come to $990,445.54. He wanted the thrill of having an even million in his hand.

They don't make boxing checks like that any more.

There was one other reason why a third fight between Tunney and me never came off. Tex Rickard, as I said, was a peculiar kind of guy. He wasn't thinking so much about a rematch as about giving some new fellow a chance to prove he had the right to fight Gene. He thought up an elimination tournament to pick the right fellow, and I don't remember feeling hurt about that. I wasn't hurt because he did me the honor of making me his partner.

I was as proud of that as of anything in my life. When I was a bum being trucked through Goldfield in a wheelbarrow after my fight with Johnny Sudenberg, Tex had been far beyond me, the promoter of fights so big I could hardly understand them. Now there was his big hand shaking mine, and he was telling me I was his fifty-fifty partner until death.

We never had a contract. You didn't need one with Tex Rickard.

He was the great man of my life.

They don't make them like Rickard any more. He wore a half-Texas hat and he had a half-Texas way of talking. He was a bourbon-and-branch-water man who could drink all night and not get drunk. He had the big, clear, cold gray eyes of the good gambler he was. He talked like a man who spent most of his life in high-stake poker games— short sentences, and let's get on with the game, boys. He was a gambler of the old school. He bet high with cards and dice where there wasn't any kidding about it, in the gold fields of Alaska and California and Nevada. He bet on guarantees to fighters.

Tex always claimed he remembered me from Goldfield as a "pore skinny-looking thing got wheelbarrowed home."

He didn't know me from then. We first got real friendly at Toledo. He spent a lot of time out at the training camp with me.

"Now, you get in real good shape, son," he'd say. "You work hard and you might beat that big feller." He was afraid Willard would kill me.

It was a little thing for a promoter to say, I guess, but I was mighty grateful. I hadn't met any promoters before who gave a good damn whether I lived or croaked.

Tex had raised cattle in Paraguay and Bolivia, been a sheriff in a tough Texas frontier town, and mixed with some of the toughest characters, from guys out of the Old West with guns to the Tommy-gun guys Al Capone had on his payroll. He was always ready for any of them. He outsmarted some of the most larcenous guys in the history of boxing and outtoughed some of the toughest.

People forget that his name was George, just like they forget that Babe Ruth's name was George. George wasn't right for either of them. George Rickard? George Ruth? Somebody gave them righter names.

Tex was born in Kansas City, Missouri, in either 1870 or 1872. When he was four years old his folks moved to Sherman, Texas. He was a working cow hand when he was ten, town marshal of Henrietta, Texas, when he was twenty-three. He came down with gold fever in 1895 and took off for the Klondike. He couldn't find gold but he found something that paid even better, a gambling hall that took the gold the other guys panned or dug.

Hype Igoe, Jim Dawson and the other great old New York boxing writers used to give Tex the bird when he said, "I ran the only honest game up there. Went broke many a night. It was the dealers, not so much the players, who used to murder me. Dealers from them other places. When they was through work they'd all come over and take a crack at my games. "Boys, any time you're in a strange town and you want to gamble, gamble where the dealers gamble. They know where the honest game is."

Tex must have had some good nights in Alaska, too. He told me once that at one time he had half a million dollars. But the same guy who had taken what the miners brought in to him, to gamble, gambled the half million on a lot of gold claims that never panned out. He blew it all and headed south broke. He worked around San Francisco for a time, doing cheap jobs, for him, and then headed into the Nevada hills to Goldfield.

Goldfield wanted to be important, wanted to be ahead of Tonopah and even Reno. Somebody asked Tex if he had any ideas on what might put the town across. Tex had a good idea. He had a saloon by now. He got together $30,000 in gold and put it in the window of his saloon and announced to the *Police Gazette*, and things like that, that he was interested in giving the gold to any two "name" fighters who'd come to Goldfield and fight.

The money attracted Bat Nelson and Joe Gans. They fought forty-three rounds in the broiling sun, with Gans winning in the forty-third on a foul. To everybody's surprise, except maybe Tex's, Tex made $30,000 on the fight.

In 1910 Jim Jeffries answered the pleas of all the people who believed in "white supremacy" and decided to come back and fight Jack Johnson. Half a dozen of the country's top promoters met in Reno to bid for the fight. Finally it got up to $81,000— the most money, by far, that had ever been guaranteed for a fight. Rickard hadn't taken any part in the bidding until now, when it looked like nobody would or could top $81,000. Then he spoke up and offered $101,000. He had it with him in cash. He got the fight, as you know.

Then South America for six years. In 1918 he was in New York and raised $15,000 to rent Madison Square Garden for a night to show Jess Willard, then champion, against Frank Moran. In the years after that, of course, he became the top fellow at the Garden, raised the millions that built the new Garden, ran boxing and nearly everybody in it, including me. Which suited me.

In some ways, Tex was the biggest sucker I ever met. He knew all the angles, had been everywhere and done everything, could spot a phony at five hundred yards, but anybody could sell him stock in an undrilled oil well or any other get-rich-quick idea. I never had dinner with him that he wasn't all excited over some new invention a guy was being kind enough to let him in on.

For all his savvy, he must have gone for a lot, here and there. I know he did on his last big fight— Tunney against Tom Heeney in June of 1928. His boxing-writer friends had told him it would be a turkey, but Gene didn't think so and neither did his rich friends, and that was good enough for Tex. The fight drew $691,014, out of which had to be deducted things like state and Federal taxes coming to nearly $150,000, ball park rental $50,000, tickets and carpentry and publicity $60,000, and so on. Tunney was guaranteed and got $625,000, Heeney $100,000. Tex and the Garden blew at least a quarter of a million that night. But there were a lot of other losses too. There must have been. In an interview not long before he died he told a sports writer he was worth $2,500,000, with a million of it in cash. But all we found when he died was peanuts.

Rickard bet on his own opinion once too often, and it cost me my partnership with him only three months after we sealed it with a handshake. But that was nothing. It cost Tex his life. He bet his life he could beat appendicitis without an operation. He died in a Miami hospital in January 1929. He was either fifty-seven or fifty-nine.

I was about the only guy he'd see near the end. I flew to Miami from Detroit, raced to the hospital, and there he was, weak from the emergency operation they had finally done on him after knocking him out.

"Jack," he said, "this is gonna be okay. I don't want to talk too much now. I got it licked. When I want you I'll call you."

He wanted me and called me later in the day, and died in my arms.

I called his mother to tell her Tex was dead, then his wife arranged to order the body sent to New York. If there was going to be a funeral it should be from Madison Square Garden, I figured.

He had a funeral they're still talking about. They lost count of the number of people who went past the coffin when his body lay in state on the floor of the Garden, just where the ring sits.

He had gone to Miami to promote the Jack Sharkey–

Billy Kid Stribling fight. I took it over as promoter, in Tex's name. It made out all right but not because of anything I could do. It made out because Tex had made the match and the people knew it was okay if it had his stamp on it— the stamp of the greatest fight promoter of all time. And as great a man as I ever met.

CHAPTER **17**

WHEN THE BOOK WAS CLOSED ON MY
recognized fight life it showed I had had sixty-nine fights,
knocked out forty-seven opponents, won seven decisions,
won once by a foul, had five no-decision fights, lost four
decisions and got knocked out once.

I should've left it at that, but four or five years later, in the middle of the depression, I needed money all over again. I went out and got it the only way I knew. Between August 20, 1931, and August 15, 1932, I fought 175 guys, sometimes as many as four a night. I knocked out more than a hundred of them, and there were a lot of people around who kept telling me that I could become the first heavyweight who ever won back the title he had lost. Jack Sharkey was champion.

For a time there I almost got talked into it. I was thirty-seven. The ham-donnies I was fighting were falling over like tenpins. Boxing writers were saying— at least the younger ones were— that I was hitting as hard as I had hit nine years before, the night I got paid $120,000 a minute (as somebody figured out) for belting Firpo for a little under four minutes.

Just then, in August 1932, a lucky thing happened to me. Kingfish Levinsky slapped me all over the ring in four rounds. I knew it was time to hang them up for keeps.

If I had ever been sap enough to get in there with Sharkey, at thirty-seven, he probably would have knocked me out, and that would have been no way to end a career.

As it turned out, people even forgot that 1931–1932 "comeback." They remember me from the "long count" fight. And a lot of them, God bless 'em, still think I was robbed.

A Tunney, with his education and interests, can get far away from the ring once he leaves. But a fellow like myself hasn't a chance— even if he wants to.

I worked with Tex until his death, for myself as a promoter, and for a list of bankroll people as long as your arm. I promoted the Max Baer–Max Schmeling fight in New York in June 1933, a great fight which put Baer in line for the title he won so soon from Primo Carnera and blew so soon after to Jim Braddock.

Boxing stays awful good to me. And so do the people who are in it or connected with it. It's a nice feeling, at sixty-four, and forty years after having won the title, to have a classy fellow like Frank Graham of the New York *Journal American* write a column like this:

THE ETERNAL CHAMPION

More than 500 Swedes met the plane at the Roslanda Airport, the paper said, and gave more attention to Jack Dempsey than they did to Ingemar Johansson. It figured. It wasn't because the Swedes were accustomed to seeing Johansson and never had seen Dempsey before. No matter where he goes or whose company he is in, everybody gives more attention to Dempsey than to anyone else. If he'd gone to Sogne, Norway, instead of to Goteborg to preside over the Johansson–Patterson rematch plans, he would have stolen the show from the Rockefeller–Rasmussen wedding.

Ingo merely learned what other champions have learned before him, which is that champions come and champions go, but Dempsey is the eternal champion, dwarfing all those who followed in his train. When Joe Louis won the title people asked themselves if he could have licked Dempsey. When Rocky Marciano was at his peak, they asked if he could have licked Dempsey. Forgotten in their speculations was that Gene

Tunney had licked Dempsey not once but twice. Gene only licked Dempsey. He didn't succeed him. When he retired he became just another ex-champion, while Dempsey carried on, the mob still at his heels.

There never has been any one like him in prize fight history, not even John L. Sullivan, first of the great mauling heroes, whose defeat by James J. Corbett in 1892 was so bitterly resented across the nation that Corbett emerged as a villain from the Battle of New Orleans. Sullivan's popularity endured among his followers but to the generations rising about him he was little more than a museum piece and it was difficult for them to vizualize in this gray, portly preacher against the evils of alcohol the trim, black-haired Boston Strong Boy who bragged that he could lick any --- -- - ----- in the world, that their fathers remembered so well.

Dempsey won the championship by battering Jess Willard into submission at Toledo, Ohio, on July 4, 1919, or slightly more than 40 years ago. He lost it to Tunney in 1926 and failed to regain it in another whirl with Gene in 1927 and that was 32 years ago. Generations rising about him, too, as they did about John L., have seen him, even met him. But this is no old one they have looked upon, this hero of their fathers. There's a light frosting gathering on his full head of dark hair but the face still is the face of Dempsey. He's put on weight, but his body still is hard and he still walks quickly.

"There goes Jack Dempsey!" they say, wherever he goes, and he's still Dempsey.

And when they meet him, he goes more than half way to meet them. Dempsey, the natural one, still talking like a guy straight out of Manassa, Colo., still unspoiled by his years in the kind of prominence that has ruined so many others. With him it's "how're you, pardner?" or "how're you, pal?" And there is nothing phony about his greeting because he genuinely likes to meet people. How does he stand it, this never ending contact with his public? Because he's Dempsey.

The first time Dempsey met Johansson was when Ingo was training at Grossinger's for the Patterson fight. The setting was the plush ranch house, privately owned, where Ingo and his entourage were quartered. They stood there, on the terrace, shaking hands, smiling at each other, and they seemed, at the moment, as a boy meeting a man and, in the background, someone murmured:

"I'll lay 8 to 5 Dempsey could lick him."

"Dempsey couldn't, of course," somebody else said.

"Not in the ring," the other said, "but put them together in a small room, and I'd have to take Dempsey."

Right or wrong, there it was again. Dempsey, champion of the world.

Dempsey left to get into his car and be driven back to Grossinger's.

"He is my father's hero," Ingo said.

"And your own?"

"Joe Louis was my hero when I was growing up," Ingo said, "but my father always talked to me about Dempsey."

Dempsey's car was being wheeled down the driveway and Ingo looked after it. There was something in his eyes that might have made you believe he might have been thinking his father was right, after all.

I keep thinking of the good ones who wound up with

nothing, except maybe clippings. Like Langford, the man I was afraid to fight as a kid, and the great old middleweight whose name I took.

Jack Dempsey the Nonpareil's actual name was Kelly. He was a poor immigrant Irish kid around New York in 1883 when he got into boxing by accident. The headliner on a show he had bought a seat for failed to show up and the promoter took Kelly as a volunteer substitute— and introduced him as "Jack Dempsey."

The "Nonpareil" was made up by the sports writers, and he rated it. He beat more than sixty straight opponents between 1883 and 1888, from welterweights to heavyweights, and never weighed more than 150. In 1889 he lost to George La Blanche in San Francisco in a fight that you still hear about. In the twenty-second round La Blanche stuck his right arm and fist straight out, spinning around as fast as he could, and it connected with Dempsey's jaw— making Dempsey the first and I guess only victim of the pivot punch. It was banned immediately afterward.

But the Nonpareil was never the same after that. He lost his title to Bob Fitzsimmons, bummed around here and there, picked up a little money at a benefit in New York, headed west with it, died and was forgotten until a Portland, Oregon, lawyer who had known him found his grave and wrote the greatest poem boxing ever knew. Every time I read it I think to myself, That could mean *me*. It goes:

> *Far out in the wilds of Oregon,*
> *On a lonely mountainside,*

Where Columbia's mighty waters
    Roll down to the ocean side;
Where the giant fir and cedar
    Are imaged in the waves,
O'ergrown with firs and lichens,
    I found Jack Dempsey's grave.

I found no marble monolith
    No broken shaft, or stone,
Recording sixty victories,
    This vanquished victor won;
No rose, no shamrock, could I find
    No mortal here to tell
Where sleeps in this forsaken spot
    Immortal Nonpareil.

A winding wooded canyon road
    That mortals seldom tread,
Leads up this lonely mountain
    To the desert of the dead.
And the Western sun was sinking
    In Pacific's golden wave
And those solemn pines kept watching
    Over poor Jack Dempsey's grave.

Forgotten by ten thousand throats,
    That thundered his acclaim,
Forgotten by his friends and foes,
    Who cheered his very name.
Oblivion wraps his faded form

But ages hence shall save
The memory of that Irish lad
That fills poor Dempsey's grave.

Oh, Fame, why sleeps thy favored son
In wilds, in woods, in weeds,
And shall he ever thus sleep on,
Interred his valiant deeds?
'Tis strange New York should thus forget
Its bravest of the brave
And in the fields of Oregon,
Unmarked, leave Dempsey's grave.

They can forget you, too.

At least, my wives could.

Hannah Williams and I were married in 1933, a year after Miss Taylor and I were divorced. Hannah was a beautiful girl with a good voice, a lively personality, and a national reputation for singing "Cheerful Little Earful." When it came to my asking her to marry me I couldn't forget that Miss Taylor's career problems had busted us up. So I laid it on the line with Hannah. I wanted a home and kids, not a life of hanging around a stage door or a movie lot, waiting for her to get off work.

That's just what she wanted too, Hannah said. And for a long time she lived up to it just wonderfully. We lived in New York in a penthouse on top of the Hotel Great Northern, which I controlled for a time. Everything was great. Joan was born at Polyclinic in 1935, Barbara in the same hospital two years later.

Would I have wanted a boy? Sure. Every father wants a son, no matter what he tells you. If I had had a boy would I have wanted him to be a fighter? I don't know. If I had had a son and he wanted to fight, I wouldn't have stopped him. But I kind of think that things I would have done for him while he was growing up would have led him into something else. I would have wanted him to go to the best schools, to a good university, and take an interest in other sports. It's a cinch that all these things would have led him away from the ring. You get your good fighters mainly out of families and racial groups that are poor, underprivileged and without much schooling. Just look back in the record books. When the Irish were poor in this country, fresh off the boat, the ring was filled with good Irish fighters. Then as the second generation and the third generation came along and got better schooling, better living conditions, they began disappearing from fighting. They were followed by the Italian fighters, then by the good Jewish fighters. The Jews were replaced by the Negro fighters, and now the Puerto Ricans are coming along real strong— because they're the new underprivileged class.

So maybe Jack Dempsey, Jr., would have tried his hand at something else. Ty Cobb was the roughest, toughest, meanest ballplayer I ever saw. Ty Cobb, Jr., turned out to be a nice tennis player.

As long as I live I'll be grateful to Hannah for giving me my wonderful girls.

Shortly after Barbara was born her mother decided that she had to go back into show business. Boredom? The ham in her? Who knows? I never did. And back she went.

But, exactly like the case of Miss Taylor, Hannah's new bookings were a disappointment to her. It was my fault, it seems.

The girls were small and needed good attention as we started to crack up, and they weren't getting it. A crazy nursemaid Hannah hired once fed them dozens of aspirin tablets "to keep them from crying at night."

Hannah decided that every night club in New York was a home away from home. It finally got to be a case of my bringing a sensational divorce action with a photographer and a couple of witnesses. It was a job that made me sick, but it had to be done for my girls.

A Catholic convent was their real mother during the rest of their growing years.

Of course, it happened in Los Angeles. So much did in my life and still does.

I finally got Bernie to settle down there. Good old Bernie opened a gym and managed a few fighters. Bernie was never what you'd call a city boy. For instance, he could never understand the ways of publicity as long as he lived. One year Knute Rockne brought his Notre Dame football team to L.A. The boys wanted to visit Bernie's gym to watch the fighters. They came to me about it and I took up the matter with Bernie.

"That's fifty cents a man, you know, to get in," he said.

"Aw, c'mon, Bernie," I said, "these are college kids. It'll be good publicity for the joint— pictures and things like that."

He wasn't so sure. But finally he shrugged. "How many guys on a football team, Harry?" he asked me.

"Eleven."

That was my mistake. Twenty-five, about half of Rockne's squad, showed up. Bernie let in the first eleven guys for nothing. Then he charged the rest of them fifty cents a head.

Another time, Bernie loaned a fellow some money. The fellow was slow paying it back. Finally he promised to get it up the following day, but instead he blew it gambling. Bernie went to his hotel and hit the guy on the head with a water pitcher. "Don't break no promises to me," he said, like a lecturer. Bernie was a wonderful character.

Joe Dempsey did okay in Los Angeles, too. He's the quiet Dempsey. No water pitchers on the skull. Joe was a successful real-estate operator in Los Angeles for years; manages an apartment house for me.

For me, as I said, L.A. has had its ups and its downs. My kids and their children live there, so I'll never get very far away for very long. I knew and know some of the most colorful characters the town ever had, men like Wilson Mizner, Baron Long, John Considine, Joe Schenck, W. C. Fields, John Barrymore, Dave Chasen, Mike Romanoff, Gene Fowler and a thousand others.

New York's my legal home, but when I drive somewhere in New York it's just a drive. When I drive somewhere in Los Angeles— anywhere— it brings back memories. Some of them are sad and bitter, some full of laughs and sweet. The big towns of my life have been New York, San Francisco, Salt Lake City and L.A. I was a bum in all of them except Los Angeles, where I was always in the money but not always in the race.

CHAPTER **18**

IT WILL NEVER BE LISTED IN NAT
Fleischer's *All-Time Ring Record Book*, but I've had a lot
of fights ever since the day, more than twenty-five years
ago, when my name first appeared over a restaurant door.
The average customer at Dempsey's, both when it was
on Eighth Avenue opposite Madison Square Garden and

since it's been in the heart of Broadway, has been kind, considerate, and even flattering enough to ask for my autograph. But there's always a fellow who wants to take a punch at an ex-pugilist proprietor, especially if the proprietor ever held a title. Every fighter who ever opened a place that sold whisky has found this to be true.

I don't know what it is, but there it is. Maybe guys like that want to go back home the next day and gather the boys around and say, "Well, I took a punch at Jack Dempsey last night . . ."

Although at least a hundred of them have swung at me in the years I've been in business, only a dozen or so have connected. Most of these were decent people with no experience, such as I had, at saloon fighting. The sign of the amateur saloon fighter is that he talks. He always tells you in advance what he thinks he's going to do.

The pros, if there are such things any more, throw the punch and discuss the matter later. They're pretty easy to duck, or what they throw at you doesn't matter too much, for they're generally out of condition. Amateur or pro, I've formed the habit of laughing at them and showing them to the door— though I'll bet that through the years I've lost an awful lot of fights in my joints, according to the stories the boys carried back home.

This crazy urge that so often descends on meek and mild guys to belt a prize fighter isn't restricted to the boxer in his restaurant. It can happen in places where his name isn't over the door, too. I was promoting for a chocolate company once and my travels took me to a cocktail party in Buffalo. I was introduced to a big, nice-looking banker. He shook hands, looked at the pale Scotch and soda I had in my hand and said, "I never touch that stuff, Mr. Dempsey."

I congratulated him. I seldom do, either.

Unfortunately, I also believed him. He was back half an hour later. I could see he had been hitting the stuff he had warned me about.

"So, you're the champ, eh?" he said.

"Not lately," I said.

He hit me with a perfect right to the jaw. Then he fell flat on his face. I hadn't even moved. He had simply passed out with the final effort of throwing his punch.

I met him the next day at a luncheon. "Mr. Dempsey," he said, "I'll never forgive myself for what happened last night. My friends tell me I struck you. Believe me, I had never had a drink in my life before meeting you."

I said, "Aw, hell, forget it."

But he kept apologizing. Over and over. At last I managed to convince him that I had no hard feelings, that I had forgotten all about it. He shook hands again, started away and came back at me. I figured he was going to try another shot, so I put up a kind of defense.

But all he wanted to do was ask me a question. "Tell me the truth, Mr. Dempsey. Can I really punch hard?"

I told him I hadn't been hit so hard since Firpo slugged me. How could I tell him he punched like a banker?

One night a fellow came into my place on Broadway, pulled out a gun and chased me all over the joint. When the cops finally cooled him off he turned out to be an escaped mental patient.

There have been troubles occasionally with people who demanded a yes or no answer, right off, to the question, "You don't remember me, do you?"

I don't think anybody who has been in the public eye for as long as I have can remember good enough to suit people. My old friend Jim Farley is unquestionably the best I've ever seen at coming up with a name, but sometimes Jim fails too, and he has friends who say that his great memory is just a fraud. Bugs Baer says that the way Jim gets the name is to keep shaking hands with the stranger and slapping him on the back with the other hand all the while he's telling him how glad he is to see him.

"Eventually," Bugs says, "the bum's calling card will pop out of his vest and Jim's got his name."

I guess over the years I've met fifty people a day. That's conservative, of course. But let's say fifty. Since the Fulton fight that would mean about a million people. It has been a lot more. Univac, or whatever they call it, couldn't keep track of that many.

What I do to the fellow who grabs me by the lapels and gives me the "You don't remember me, do you?" business is say, "Sure, pardner," and stall around a bit, hoping he'll tip his mitt. If he tells me his home town I'm usually home free— if I don't remember him I'll usually know somebody he knows or knew, for there aren't many towns in the U.S. I haven't been in.

I remember one guy of this type with great respect after twenty years and more. He saw me glad-handing people in my restaurant and struggling now and then to remember where I had met a customer. He came over to me, pushed his way through the crowd, stuck out his duke and said, "You don't remember me, do you, Jack?"

"Sure, pal," I said. "Wasn't you— "

He cut me off with a laugh.

"Jack, you're a lying old bastard," he said. "We never met in our lives."

I shook hands with him gratefully.

This attempt to make people feel I really remember meeting them maybe thirty or forty years before has two sides when I succeed. First, it's nice when I really do. They feel good about it and so do I. Second, it can be expensive. You can't refuse to cash a check for a fellow you remember meeting at a Willie Meehan fight, can you? I've got a bathroom papered with rubber checks, including one that was dated eighteen years before the night I cashed it.

It may surprise many, but I'm not just a front for my restaurant or any of my other businesses. I like to keep active in all of them, from Broadway to my interests in Palm Springs and Hesperia, California. In the long run, I think active participation has paid off. There are exceptions, of course, such as the night I overruled my cashier at the restaurant and insisted that a guest whose looks I didn't like had given him a phony $50 bill in payment of a $40 check. I called the cops— and settled the case out of court for $1,500.

When the spotlight's on you, you never can be sure who may come in from out of the dark and sell you a bill of goods.

I was standing in front of the restaurant one afternoon

years ago when a seedy-looking old guy came up to me.
He remembered me from an hour I spent in Atlantic City.

"I think you should be a fight promoter, now that Tex
Rickard's dead," he said.

I said, "Thanks, pardner, I've got to see a fellow . . ."
But he had me by the arm.

"I've got fifty thousand to put you in business."

I looked at him. "Thanks, pal. I gotta run now."

He took a fresh hold on me and stuck his face close to
me. "You think I'm a bum, don't you?"

I'm usually a patient guy. But this time I said, "Yeah,
now that you mention it, I'd say you were a bum."

"I've got fifty thousand dollars that says I'm no bum," he
yelled, and he stuck his hand in his pocket and came out
with the money. It was a threadbare pocket, too.

I took him to my lawyer. The lawyer checked him out
and he had fine business connections in Atlantic City. We
set up a promoting business with me as promoter and Jack
Fugazy, who had been second only to Tex in the good
days, as the matchmaker. We were going to operate in
New York and Chicago. We started planning to put on
a fight in Chicago.

My pal came to me about this time and said his organ-
ization wasn't immediately ready to carry the enterprise
on its books, so what about putting it in my name? I said
sure. Not long after that I picked up a paper one day and
there was his face staring at me— he was under indictment
in Atlantic City for embezzlement. Eventually he went to
jail. Deals had been made in my name, and when the
smoke cleared I was clipped for $100,000.

It doesn't matter what his name was.

But I can tell you the name of another fellow who "hustled" me. His name was Bobby Manziel. One day in the late 'twenties I got a wire from Bobby putting the bite on me for $400. I couldn't place the name for a bit, then remembered a nice little guy who had barnstormed with me years before, fighting a little, refereeing a little and chauffeuring a lot. I sent him the $400.

During the depression, when everybody could use a buck, I got a check from Manziel. It was for $100. Then another one came for $180. Then one for $210. Then one for $500. I sent him a wire asking him if he had gone nuts.

Bobby had struck oil. That $400 became, without question, the best investment I ever made.

A couple of years before Bobby died he said to me, "Jack, you're wearing yourself out, bouncing around the country, refereeing rassling matches and things like that. Why don't you settle down someplace and relax?"

I told him the truth. "I love it, Bobby," I said. "I'll never settle down."

"Tell you what," he said. "I'll give you fifty thousand dollars a year salary just to stay in Texas and play pinochle with me."

Just some faces in what has become a pretty big crowd in my mind. Good people, most of them, young and old. The little girls who ask for an autograph today, because of something their parents or even their grandparents may have told them, always remind me of my own daughters at that age. The boys who step up, menu or autograph book in hand, pen ready, remind me that for all these statistics about juvenile delinquency and the number of crimes committed by young hoodlums, ninety-nine out of every hundred boys and young men I meet are perfect gentlemen.

I wish I had been as classy when I was a kid.

CHAPTER **19**

MAURIE WAXMAN, MY BUSINESS MAN-
ager for many years, was a tough-looking fellow. But he
had a big heart. He also had a big razor scar reaching
down one side of his head. Somebody had cut him by
mistake years before.

Maurie was a good idea man. One hot day in 1942 he

and I were sitting in the restaurant when he got one of the best ideas of his life.

"Let's join the Army, Jack," he said. He was fat and in his middle fifties. I was plump, let's say, and forty-seven.

"I'm ready," I said.

We got up and walked out of the place and down Broadway to the recruiting booth at Times Square. The heat was coming out of the pavement in waves that made you dizzy.

A kid behind the counter looked us over and sent us downtown to the Whitehall Building near the southern tip of Manhattan. The colonel in charge seemed confused, but he was cordial enough.

"We're tickled to death to have you, Mr. Dempsey," he said. He looked at Maurie and, after a little bit, said, "And you too, Mr. Waxman."

We took our physicals. And that was the end of Maurie's military career— and the beginning of mine. I passed. An Army photographer came in all out of breath. The more pictures he took of me the more uneasy I got.

I asked to see the colonel once more, and when he let me in I said, "Colonel, sir, please don't release the story or those pictures to the papers until you're sure everything is okay. I had a little trouble once, years ago. I don't want people to think it's just an act. I want to join, but I want to be damn sure the thing is for real this time, not just for a picture."

"Don't worry, Mr. Dempsey," he said to me. "We won't put you on the spot. I'm certain everything will be okay." He said he'd let me know and told me to go home.

I went back to the restaurant. That night, when the tabloids came up with their first editions, there was the picture of me, big as life. I guessed Washington had waived my age.

I packed some things the next day and reported to Whitehall Street. They took me right in to the colonel. His face was a mile long.

"I've got bad news for you," he said. "You *are* too old. The Army won't take you."

"What about those damn pictures I told you not to put in the paper?" I asked him.

"I can only apologize for that," he said. "I thought it was a one hundred per cent sure thing that they'd waive the forty-five-year rule for you."

My ten-minute career in the Army gave some writers with long memories a chance to bring up the "slacker" stories of the previous World War. I was sick. The only consolation I had was that Barbara and Joan were too young to read.

A few days later a hunting and fishing expert friend of mine, Bob Edge, came into the restaurant. He was in Coast Guard uniform and had a Coast Guard commander with him. I was still steaming about what had happened to me with the Army.

"Are you really serious about wanting to get into the service?" the Coast Guard commander asked me.

"Of course I am," I said.

He whipped out some papers and said, "Sign here, then."

I signed up. I spent that following weekend with some friends of mine in Long Branch, New Jersey, and while there received a wire ordering me to appear at 9 A.M. Monday morning at 25 Whitehall Street to be sworn in as a lieutenant in the U.S. Coast Guard. I was there on time, and twelve hours later I was on a plane flying to Denver.

The first job they gave me was refereeing a fight in connection with a War Bond rally. That started two weeks of appearances at bond rallies all over the West. I did everything they asked me, but I wished like hell that it was something closer to the war.

Then I was assigned to Manhattan Beach Coast Guard Station, Brooklyn. It was the biggest Coast Guard base in the U.S. and housed as many as fifteen thousand men in boot training. I was ordered to set up and train a 500-man Shore Police unit.

"What?" I said to the commander who gave me the order. I didn't know how policemen operated. At least, not from the policeman's viewpoint. They might just as well have told me to instruct five hundred surgeons or radar men or something.

After three or four days I was called to the office of the base commander, Captain Stewart. He chewed me out real good for sitting on my tail and doing nothing. I'd been chewed out before, but what hurt this time was when he said, "Dempsey, I thought you joined to help."

"Listen, I did," I said, forgetting the "sir" and all that. "But I don't know a damn thing about police work. The only thing I know something about is getting men in shape. And teaching them how to protect themselves."

He looked at me for some time, then smiled. He was a kind guy, really.

"Okay, Jack," he said. "Forget about this."

A couple days later I was put in charge of the physical-fitness program on the base. My assistant was Spike Mooney of the Ohio State football coaching staff. With Spike's help I got my hands on a lot of old fighters and rasslers now in the Coast Guard and ordered them to come to a meeting.

"Listen, you guys," I said, looking out over them, "I'm the boss. My first order is that when we're working together, training these guys, I'm 'Jack.' When the brass is around I'm 'Lieutenant.' We're going to teach these kids how to protect themselves, in case it ever comes down to whether they got to kill or get killed."

It was all I had to say, but they just sat there waiting for some more.

"Who's got the cards?" was all I could think to say.

All of them seemed to have a deck.

I had a great outfit. You could tell one of my men from a hundred yards away. I guess I commanded the most busted noses and tin ears in military history.

My boys showed the kids how to fight like you'd have to fight in a jungle or a saloon. Of course, when there was an inspection and when the photographers were around we filled the rings with good-looking young boys boxing my tin-eared guys. Everybody then would box beautifully, and it didn't do any harm. But when we were working alone with the kids we taught them the facts of life, the facts of survival in a war where no holds were going to be barred. World War II wasn't a war where a fight started after a fellow said to the enemy, "Put up your hands and fight like a man, you cad." I'm pretty sure we saved some lives by that training.

I had Lou Ambers and Marty Servo, ex-champs and fine gents, on my staff. Also Bibber McCoy, who had clowned around the rassling circuit for years, but who knew holds and moves that could kill a man. After watching Bibber level I knew why rassling could never be honest. All the contestants would soon be disabled or dead.

That wasn't the only job I had at Manhattan Beach. I doubled as a mess officer (somebody heard I had met the chef of my Broadway place), served as a court-martial board officer, and had something to do with the officers' club. But at heart, like a lot of other guys in service, particularly the older ones, I was all civilian. It didn't seem to make too much sense for guys my age and older to jump off buildings in training just because eighteen-year-old kids were expected to.

There were a lot of kids in that camp while I was there, and most of them were lonely— which was the case everywhere else, of course. Some of them seemed to get a kick out of coming up, shaking hands with me and talking about fights I had had before they were born. That suited me, naturally. If they got a kick out of shaking hands with an old fighter and writing home that they had, well, I was ready, willing and eager.

One day when I was doing this kind of thing, a lieutenant broke up the crowd and gave me a loud dressing down in front of the kids, for "shaking hands with enlisted men." It was embarrassing to the kids and to me. I often wondered what would have happened if I had belted him. For his own sake in later life.

He was an exception, of course. A vast majority of the men I met in service were just great. One of them was the Beach's morale officer, a nice guy named Hickey. One day he came to me and said, "Jack, we oughtta have a grand opening for our new gym here. Can you help us?"

"Sure," I said. Right off I thought that a good show, with a lot of pretty girls and some Broadway talent I might scrounge, could do the job. I went to my office and put in a call for a couple of show girls I knew could help me get that part of it going. They said they'd be happy to come out and discuss it with me.

Well, the next day in the pouring rain I got a call from the guard at the main gate that two unauthorized females were there, demanding to see me. I told him to let them pass and send them to my office, but he wouldn't. So I went right to the gate, pulled what little rank I had and brought them in.

We talked the matter over and lined up a show, and they were about to leave when one of my broken-nosed instructors came in, saluted like somebody in *Beau Geste* and said, "Jack, you better hide them broads."

"Why?"

"The joint's crawling with brass from Washington," he said. "Big unexpected inspection."

The best place to hide the girls, of course, was to keep them there in my little office.

It was a cold, raw day and the weather had seeped into

my little room. One of the girls began to sniffle with a head cold. She had brought along her own medicine, a pint of whisky in her purse. The other girl just happened to have a deck of cards with her. So we settled down with the whisky and the cards to wait for the brass to return to Washington and for the coast to clear. The girl with the head cold got colder. She decided to sit on my lap.

That's about when it happened. Captain Stewart, it seems, wanted to show the Washington brass his Lieutenant Dempsey. He came in without knocking. It was like a scene from Sergeant Bilko.

"What's going on here?" he roared.

I got up and saluted, using the other hand to keep the girl with the head cold from taking a prat fall.

"Sir, these are girls— "

"Really!" he said.

"Yes, sir. They are girls who are down here on business— "

"I don't doubt that one little bit! Now get them off this base!"

"But they're here to help the men— "

"Get them off!"

"Yes, sir."

I took them to the gate, got them transportation and came back to my office. There was a summons there to report to Captain Stewart.

"Lieutenant Dempsey, are you the commandant of this base?" he asked me. I had a hunch he knew the answer.

"No, sir."

"Are you aware that I gave orders today that no civilians

were to be admitted to the base, yet you pushed away a sentry obeying those orders?"

"Aw, I didn't push him, Captain. I just didn't listen to him. You know how it is."

He didn't. He took a long time telling me that I wasn't running the base, and who was. I agreed on all points. Then he barked at me, "Furthermore, what was in that bottle?"

"One of the girls had a very bad cold, sir."

"Hmmm, and what is all that red stuff on your face?"

I didn't know there was. "I guess when you came in you surprised me so much that when I turned around to see who it was my face must've brushed against the girl's lips. You know, the girl right beside me."

"Right beside you on your lap! Don't give me that stuff, Lieutenant. Dismissed!"

I saluted, turned and started out.

"Lieutenant!" Captain Stewart said, stopping me. I wondered what he could have overlooked.

"Yes, sir."

"Those two girls . . . ahem. Very pretty girls."

Captain Stewart made me understand the meaning of "an officer and a gentleman."

It says in the regulations that an officer must know how to navigate. Even an officer who learned all his mathematics at the Lakeview Grammar School in Utah. So I was ordered to navigation school.

The kid who was our instructor was a real brain. And I felt as dumb as I had felt back in Provo, and was.

» 237 «

"This is a fine Saturday," he said one morning, "so no lecture. No questions. Instead I'm going to put ten problems on the blackboard. When a man solves them he can leave."

I watched him write down the ten problems and said, "Good God, I'll be here forty years!"

I didn't mean to say it so loud.

After that, the Coast Guard got me a tutor and he was on my neck for six whole months. I learned a little navigation. But it was a waste of time and the taxpayers' money, because the Coast Guard was even more determined than I was that I should never command anything that didn't have at least one cauliflower ear.

But there came a day during World War II when they actually sent me to sea. I was teamed up with a wonderful guy named Harvey Twyman, a radio announcer and cameraman. Our job was morale. He took pictures of the kids with me and sent them to home-town newspapers. Or we taped interviews with boys and sent the tape to home-town radio stations.

It wasn't very heroic work. But everybody seemed to recognize me and everybody seemed glad to see me, from seaman to private to admiral to general.

I was on a ship in the Pacific one day when I overheard a Marine say to a buddy, "Hell, we ain't going nowhere. We got Jack Dempsey on board. They wouldn't take a chance on losing him, would they?"

The kid was right. We were going to a place that seemed like nowhere once we got there— Okinawa.

When I hit the beach there I was surprised to be greeted by a general, a real general.

"You're Jack Dempsey, aren't you?" he said, sizing me up.

"Yes, sir."

"Well, what the hell is an old guy like you doing here?" he said, hitting me on the back. "This stuff is for young guys."

He was a good five years older than I was.

When the fighting on Okinawa was almost over, somebody in Coast Guard public relations had a lousy idea. He said, out loud, "Why don't the Marines take Dempsey along tomorrow when they clean out a nest of Japs? We'll send along a photographer and the picture will hit every paper in the world."

When the idea got to me it came down from the top. I squawked. "For the love of God," I said, "you want those Marines to die laughing?"

But I was overruled.

The Coast Guard, quite naturally, had lost the play to the Marine Corps, and to the Navy, the Army and the Air Force, for that matter. It wanted the people back home to know that it too had been to Okinawa and was in the war. And, sad as it seemed to me, the Coast Guard casualty list wouldn't make this point as clear as a picture of me helping capture a Jap.

So we went Jap hunting, and we found a house with five of them holed up. The Marines squirted some flame at a window and they came running out in all directions.

I lit out after one of them, grabbed him by the back of

the neck. He struggled and twisted so hard that it took me ten minutes to get him under control.

The Coast Guard cameraman was there, with instructions.

"Turn him toward us, Commander," he ordered me. (I had picked up another stripe.) I turned the kicking and squirming Jap around.

The camera fellow raised his camera. Then he lowered it.

"God Almighty, Commander," he said. "That battling Jap is ninety years old."

I looked at the Jap I had captured. I had been too busy to look at him before that. He must have been at least seventy.

There were no pictures.

A few days later I got my orders to move on. I was stuffing my duffle when this kind little guy in the faded uniform, with no markings, came by and stuck out his hand.

"Goodbye, Jack," he said.

"I'll be seeing you, pardner," I said, still packing.

He stood there with a kind of grin.

"Tell me goodbye," he said. "You aren't going to see me any more."

"Aw, go on, I said, pushing him. "I'll see you someplace, like before."

He wouldn't leave me.

"Tell me goodbye, Jack," he said.

So I said goodbye to an old pal, Ernie Pyle.

I went all over the world, making tapes, posing, showing old and new fight films, explaining them, and refereeing. I even had a fight, my last one. It was in the Pacific. I refereed a fight between a green kid and a fellow who had been a pro, and gave the decision to the kid because he had earned it. The pro blew his top when I held up the kid's hand, and he got so worked up that he finally dared me to fight him.

It was crazy. You don't fight referees who make an honest decision. Besides, I was almost fifty, twice as old as this guy. But there were a lot of Coast Guard kids in the audience and they wanted me to show this fresh kid that the Coast Guard had some fighters too.

So there I was again, stripped and with the gloves on, and with a little lard around the belt.

The boy was warmed up from the previous fight, ready and willing, and knew that if he kayoed me it would mean a lot to him then and later. He gave me a hard time in the first round, but in the second he got a little careless, trying to hit me with everything he had. I got set and hit him with a left hook, and scored a knockout I could've done without.

I went wherever Coast Guard men had been sent, and they sent them everywhere. I got sick with some Asiatic growth in Ceylon and scared people, refereeing in Calcutta with all my sores. The medics ordered me home for proper treatment. It took weeks, but finally I got to Casablanca and was given a seat on a home-bound plane. What a thrill it was to take off for New York— and Barbara, Joan, some decent treatment for the sores, clean clothes, a glass of clean cold milk and all the other things a fellow looked forward to in those days. I looked around the plane and saw it filled with kids who had done much more than I had, and who had just as many reasons for wanting to get home.

Two hours out of Casablanca the big plane went into a banked turn and started back. We were all sure something was terribly wrong.

It was, too. The captain came back from the cockpit and found me. He told me he had just received instructions from his general to bring the packed plane back to Casablanca.

The general had heard I was on the plane, hadn't known I was in Casablanca, and wanted to take me hunting.

I didn't dare tell the others on the plane. But I told that general pretty good. I showed him my sores, and we were soon back in the air— headed for New York.

I was awarded European, Asiatic, Pacific and African ribbons. I was given a Legion of Merit, which was sheer insanity. When the war ended I resigned, but before the resignation went through the Coast Guard made me an offer for which I'll always be grateful. It offered me a promotion and asked that I consider making the Coast Guard my career. Captain Stewart was behind the offer. I guess my old C.O. has based my efficiency report on those wonderful kids I helped train, not on the girls I brought to his station.

These days I can't go anywhere without running into one of my old Coast Guard buddies, some of them now fat and bald and surrounded by the proud wife and kids.

I can't tell you how wonderful it makes me feel, but I guess by now you know.

INDEX

Tacoma, Washington, 54
Tate, Bill, 100
Taylor, Estelle, *see* Dempsey,
    Estelle Taylor
Tazewell, Virginia, 11
Telegram, 108
Texas Guinan's, 113, 186
The Big Fight (play), 165, 168–
    173
"The Eternal Champion" (news-
    paper story), 211–213
Toledo, Ohio, 108, 204
Tonopah, Nevada, 205
Tunney, Gene, 109, 124, 179, 190,
    191, 192–195, 198, 199–201,
    202, 203, 206–207, 210, 212
Twyman, Harvey, 238

Uncompahgre, Colorado, 18, 20,
    21–22
U. S. Coast Guard, 231, 232, 233,
    238, 240, 241, 242
U. S. District Court, San Francis-
    co, 75
U. S. Marines, 124, 239
U. S. Navy, 121, 123, 124
Universal Pictures, 188
Utica, New York, 197

Valentino, Rudolph, 110
Van Dyke, Woody, 175

Walker, James J., 116

Wallace, Marie, 115
Walla Walla, Washington, 75
Walthall, Henry B., 109
Walton, Florence, 140
Ward, Fanny, 142
Waxman, Maurie, 229–230
White, Jack, 116
Whiteman, Paul, 116
White Wolf (dog), 156
Willard, Jess, 62, 89, 92, 95, 98,
    99, 100, 101–104, 106, 107,
    108, 109, 122, 135, 147, 204,
    206, 212
Williams, Hannah, *see* Dempsey,
    Hannah Williams
Williams, Ted, 121
Wills, Harry, 179–183, 184, 190,
    196
Wilson, Gus, 160
Windsor, Fred (Windy), 76, 77,
    79–80
Wintz, George, 27, 29
Wolcott, Colorado, 20
Woods, Fred, 25, 43–44
World War I, 118, 119, 120, 121,
    122
World War II, 233, 234, 238

York, Bob, 53
Young, Tammany, 116

Ziegfeld Follies, 113, 140